PRACTICAL
GOURMET
Comp

Healthy Hor ⌐
Cooking
for Busy Families

McLaren • Paré • Darcy MAR 2017

Library and Archives Canada Cataloguing in Publication

McLaren, Sheridan, author
      Healthy home cooking : for busy families / Sheridan McLaren, Jean Paré, James Darcy.

(New original series)
Includes index.
ISBN 978-1-988133-26-3 (paperback)

      1. Cooking. 2. Cookbooks. I. Paré, Jean, author II. Darcy, James, author III. Title.

TX714.M3552 2016   641.5   C2016-906142-6

Distributed by
Canada Book Distributors - Booklogic
11414-119 Street
Edmonton. Alberta, Canada T5G 2X6
Tel: 1-800-661-9017

We acknowledge the [financial] support of the Government of Canada.

Funded by the Government of Canada
Financé par le gouvernement du Canada | Canadä

PC: 28

TABLE OF CONTENTS

Practical Gourmet

Good company and great food are a powerful combination. When laughter and conversation mix with the heady fragrance and flavours of delicious fare, we are not just sharing a meal—we are nourishing our lives. Artfully prepared dishes awaken the senses and please the palate. And here's the secret: It can be so simple!

Practical Gourmet is delighted to partner with **Company's Coming** to introduce a new series designed to help home cooks create no-fuss, sumptuous food. It is possible to wow both the eye and the palate using readily available ingredients and minimal effort. Practical Gourmet offers sophisticated recipes without the hassle of complicated methods, special equipment or obscure ingredients.

Titles in this series feature step-by-step instructions, full-page colour photos with every recipe, menu suggestions and sidebars on preparation tips and tricks.

Approachable recipe, fabulous results, wonderful get-togethers—it all starts with *Healthy Home Cooking!*

The Jean Paré Story

Jean Paré (pronounced "jeen PAIR-ee") grew up understanding that the combination of family, friends and home cooking is the best recipe for a good life. When Jean left home, she took with her a love of cooking, many family recipes and an intriguing desire to read cookbooks as if they were novels!

When her four children had all reached school age, Jean volunteered to cater the 50th anniversary celebration of the Vermilion School of Agriculture, now Lakeland College, in Alberta, Canada. Working from her home, Jean prepared a dinner for more than 1,000 people and from there launched a flourishing catering operation that continued for more than 18 years.

As requests for her recipes increased, Jean was often asked, "Why don't you write a cookbook?" The release of *150 Delicious Squares* on April 14, 1981, marked the debut of what would soon turn into one of the world's most popular cookbook series.

> "Never share a recipe you wouldn't use yourself."

Company's Coming cookbooks are distributed in Canada, the United States, Australia and other world markets. Bestsellers many times over in English, Company's Coming cookbooks have also been published in French and Spanish.

Familiar and trusted in home kitchens around the world, Company's Coming cookbooks are offered in a variety of formats. Highly regarded as kitchen workbooks, the softcover Original Series, with its lay-flat plastic comb binding, is still a favourite among home cooks.

Jean Paré's approach to cooking has always called for quick and easy recipes using everyday ingredients. That view served her well, and the tradition continues in the Practical Gourmet series.

Jean's Golden Rule of Cooking is: Never share a recipe you wouldn't use yourself. It's an approach that has worked—millions of times over!

Introduction

In today's fast-paced world, finding the time to prepare a healthy, home-cooked meal can be a challenge, and with all the pre-packaged or convenience food options on the market, many people may wonder, "why bother." Well, at Company's Coming, we believe that nothing can compare to a fresh, home-cooked meal, both in flavour and nutritional value.

Our *Healthy Home Cooking* cookbook was created for families seeking simple, nutritious, home-cooked meals. Most of the recipes can be prepared quickly and at a skill level simple enough to accommodate beginner cooks, so even kids can get involved. We've also thrown in a few more challenging dishes as well as recipes to prepare when you have a little more time on your hands. The meals in this book were created with the whole family in mind—no matter your age or food preference, there are recipes in this book you and your family will love.

In Our Kitchen

The recipes in this book are based around fresh, natural ingredients for the best possible flavour and nutrients. When sourcing your ingredients, choose the freshest ingredients you can find.

We have found the following ingredient choices and cooking procedures to be successful in our kitchen and recommend them highly wherever possible. Special ingredients found in just one or two recipes are described where they are used.

Bay Leaves—Fresh leaves have such a different flavour that they are worth the effort to find. They are occasionally available at large grocery stores and can be specially ordered. In a well-sealed container in the fridge, they can last three or four months.

Butter—Use unsalted. It is easiest to measure using the convenient markings on the wrapping.

Coconut Milk—Use unsweetened coconut milk in cans. Naturally sweet, it is often better than cream in savoury dishes.

Eggs—Use large, free-run eggs. They should be at room temperature for baking.

Flour—Use unbleached all-purpose.

Grains—Unless otherwise stated always try to source your carbohydrates—bread, pasta, rice and flours— from whole grains. Whole grain products, as the name implies, use the entire grain; whole wheat products, however, often omit parts of the grain, which are high in fibre and B vitamins.

Lemons and Limes—Use fresh! You can't compare the taste to concentrate.

Mustard—Use good quality mustard for everything from sandwiches to dressings to sauces. When you are down to the last few teaspoons clinging to the bottom of your mustard jar, add fresh lemon juice, olive oil, sea salt and fresh pepper for a yummy impromptu salad dressing. Just shake and enjoy.

Oil, Olive—Extra virgin olive oil is indispensable. Try olive oil from Italy, Spain or Greece.

Salt—Great salt is the key to great cooking. Salt brings out the flavour in food. Sea salt, kosher salt, Celtic salt—choose a favourite. Better yet, get some of each. Using a better quality salt also means that you will use less because the flavour is more intense. If you need to reduce salt even further for health reasons, use fresh herbs, various spices and flavour lifters, such as lemon juice, to maintain the flavour intensity while reducing the salt content.

Soy Sauce—Both tamari and shoyu are high quality, fermented and chemical-free "soy sauces" that enhance flavour and impart a unique saltiness.

Stocks—Nothing beats the flavour of a homemade stock, but good quality stocks available in tetra packs are the best substitute. Avoid using stocks that are high in sodium.

Sugar—Use organic and unrefined rather than white and bleached. When looking for a rich brown sugar, use muscovado sugar, available in grocery and health food stores. It still contains the minerals and vitamins originally in the sugar cane plant, and it has a full molasses flavour.

Vinegar, Balsamic—Its unique flavour is great in everything from soups to sweets. Be sure to try authentic balsamic from Modena, Italy.

Measuring

Follow recipe closely by using the proper size pots, pans and roasting trays. Each recipe has been tested in our kitchen to guarantee success when prepared according to the guidelines. Before you start cooking, have all your ingredients out and measured as well as all the tools you will need out and ready to go.

Dry ingredients should be spooned into the measuring cup and levelled off with a knife or spatula.

Measurements are in both metric and imperial. Note that for butter, a pound is considered to be 454 g; for meat, vegetables, etc., a pound is 500 g.

Solids, including butter and most cheeses, are measured in dry-measure cups and liquids in liquid-measure cups.

Creamy Guacamole with Fresh-baked Tortilla Chips

A great alternative to a bag of chips while the gang is watching the hockey game. This simple snack is loaded with essential fatty acids, calcium and magnesium.

Garlic cloves, minced	2	2
Lemon juice	1 tbsp.	15 mL
Salt	1/2 tsp.	2 mL
Pepper	1/2 tsp.	2 mL
Chili powder	1/4 tsp.	1 mL
Olive oil	2 tbsp.	30 mL
Corn tortillas (6 inch, 15 cm, diameter)	6	6
Avocadoes	2	2
Canned chickpeas, rinsed	1/4 cup	60 mL
Reserved canned chickpea liquid	1 tbsp.	15 mL
Lemon juice	1 tbsp.	15 mL
Garlic clove, minced	1	1
Chopped fresh cilantro	1 tsp.	5 mL
Cayenne pepper	1/8 tsp.	0.5 mL
Salt	1/8 tsp.	0.5 mL
Pepper	1/8 tsp.	0.5 mL
Light sour cream	1/4 cup	60 mL

In a small bowl, combine garlic, first amounts of lemon juice, salt and pepper, chili powder and oil. Brush top of each tortilla with oil mixture then cut each tortilla into 8 equal triangles. Lay chips flat on a baking sheet lined with parchment paper. Bake in 375°F (190°C) oven for 9 to 11 minutes or until chips are beginning to brown. Remove chips from oven and let cool for 10 minutes; chips will continue to darken and crisp up even after they are removed from oven.

Meanwhile, combine avocado, chickpeas, chickpea liquid and remaining lemon juice in a medium bowl and mash with a fork until smooth. Mix in garlic, cilantro, cayenne and remaining salt and pepper. Pour sour cream over top and give it a quick mix to create a swirl effect. Serve with warm chips. Makes 6 servings.

1 serving: 220 Calories; 16 g Total Fat (10 g Mono, 2 g Poly, 3 g Sat); trace Cholesterol; 18 g Carbohydrate (6 g Fibre, trace Sugar); 4 g Protein; 260 mg Sodium

Sesame Seed Hummus with Crispy Baked Pita Chips

Thick, lemony and garlicky—just like good hummus should be! It's delicious with Crispy Baked Pita Chips, or spread onto sandwiches.

19 oz. (540 mL) can of chickpeas, rinsed and drained	1	1
Olive oil	1/4 cup	60 mL
Lemon juice	2 tbsp.	30 mL
Roasted sesame seeds	2 tbsp.	30 mL
Chopped fresh parsley (or 3/4 tsp., 4 mL, flakes)	1 tbsp.	15 mL
Garlic cloves, chopped	2	2
Salt	1/2 tsp.	2 mL
Pepper	1/4 tsp.	1 mL
Garlic salt	1/2 tsp.	2 mL
Ground cumin	1/4 tsp.	1 mL
Onion powder	1/4 tsp.	1 mL
Pepper	1/4 tsp.	1 mL
Whole wheat pita breads (7 inch, 18 cm, diameter)	4	4
Cooking spray		

Process first 8 ingredients in a food processor until smooth.

Combine next 4 ingredients in a small bowl.

Carefully split pita breads. Spray inside of rounds with cooking spray. Sprinkle with garlic salt mixture. Stack rounds. Cut into 8 wedges. Arrange in a single layer on an ungreased baking sheet with sides. Bake in 350°F (175°C) oven for about 8 minutes until crisp and golden. Makes 8 servings.

1 serving: 210 Calories; 9 g Total Fat (5 g Mono, 1.5 g Poly, 1 g Sat); 0 mg Cholesterol; 28 g Carbohydrate (5 g Fibre, 1 g Sugar); 6 g Protein; 570 mg Sodium

Spinach Dip

You can drastically reduce fat and calories by using yogurt cheese as the base of this popular dip. Make sure to buy yogurt without gelatin or modified starch because those yogurts won't drain well.

Low-fat plain yogurt (no gelatin)	2 cups	500 mL
Olive (or canola) oil	1 tsp.	5 mL
Finely chopped onion	1/2 cup	125 mL
Garlic clove, minced	1	1
Hot curry powder (optional)	1/2 tsp.	2 mL
10 oz. (300 g) box of frozen spinach, thawed and squeezed dry	1	1
Salt	1/2 tsp.	2 mL
Pepper	1/4 tsp.	1 mL

Line a sieve with 3 coffee filters or a double layer of cheesecloth. Set over a large bowl. Pour yogurt into sieve and let rest in refrigerator for 12 hours. Transfer yogurt cheese to a medium bowl. Stir in 1/4 cup (60 mL) drained liquid. Discard remaining liquid.

Heat oil in a medium frying pan on medium. Add onion and cook for about 5 minutes, stirring often, until softened. Add garlic and curry powder. Heat and stir for about 1 minute until fragrant. Remove from heat.

Stir in remaining 3 ingredients. Let rest for about 15 minutes until cool. Add to yogurt cheese. Stir well. Chill, covered, for at least 1 hour. Makes about 1 3/4 cups (425 mL).

1/4 cup (60 mL): 50 Calories; 0.5 g Total Fat (0 g Mono, 0 g Poly, 0 g Sat); 0 mg Cholesterol; 8 g Carbohydrate (1 g Fibre, 5 g Sugar); 4 g Protein; 230 mg Sodium

Fiery Plantain Chips with Cocomango Dip

There are few finer delights than introducing your friends to a new taste experience—such as chili-infused plantains tempered with a cool and soothing coconut and mango dip.

Large semi-ripe plantains, peeled	2	2
Cooking oil	2 tbsp.	30 mL
Chili oil	1 tbsp.	15 mL
Chili powder	1 tsp.	5 mL
Cayenne pepper	1/2 tsp.	2 mL
Finely chopped ripe mango	1/4 cup	60 mL
Sour cream	1/4 cup	60 mL
Coconut rum	2 tbsp.	30 mL
Medium unsweetened coconut, toasted	2 tbsp.	30 mL
Sugar	1 1/2 tsp.	7 mL
Lime juice	1 1/2 tsp.	7 mL
Ground allspice	1/8 tsp.	0.5 mL
Ground nutmeg, to taste		

Cut plantain at a sharp angle into 1/8 inch (3 mm) thick slices. Combine next 4 ingredients. Add plantain and toss gently until coated. Arrange in a single layer on 2 parchment paper-lined baking sheets. Bake in 350°F (175°C) oven for 35 to 40 minutes, turning at halftime, until browned around edges. Let rest for 10 minutes.

Combine remaining 8 ingredients. Serve with chips. Makes 6 servings.

1 serving: 166 Calories; 8.0 g Total Fat (3.8 g Mono, 1.2 g Poly, 2.6 g Sat); 4 mg Cholesterol; 22 g Carbohydrate; (2 g Fibre, 12 g Sugar); 1 g Protein; 11 mg Sodium

Avocado Mango Tostadas

A delicious mix of fresh lime, creamy avocado and tangy mango on a crispy tortilla lathered with a spicy bean spread.

Corn tortillas (6 inch, 15 cm, diameter)	4	4
Olive oil	1 tbsp.	15 mL
19 oz. (540 mL) can of navy beans, rinsed and drained	1	1
Lime juice	1 tbsp.	15 mL
Olice oil	1 tbsp.	15 mL
Tex Mex seasoning	2 tsp.	10 mL
Large avocado, diced	1	1
Chopped frozen mango pieces, thawed	1 1/2 cups	375 mL
Slivered red pepper	1/2 cup	125 mL
Chopped pickled banana peppers	1/4 cup	60 mL
Thinly sliced red onion	1/4 cup	60 mL
Lime juice	2 tbsp.	30 mL
Chopped fresh cilantro	1 tbsp.	15 mL

Brush both sides of tortillas with oil. Arrange in a single layer on an ungreased baking sheet. Broil on top rack in oven for about 1 1/2 minutes per side until golden and crisp. Tortillas will crisp up more upon standing. Transfer to 4 plates.

Process next 4 ingredients in a food processor until smooth. Spread over tortillas.

Toss remaining 7 ingredients in a large bowl. Spoon avocado mixture over bean mixture. Makes 4 tostadas.

1 tostada: 290 Calories; 16 g Total Fat (10 g Mono, 2.5 g Poly, 2.5 g Sat); 0 mg Cholesterol; 37 g Carbohydrate (12 g Fibre, 11 g Sugar); 6 g Protein; 220 mg Sodium

Blackberry Mango Smoothie

Breakfast with the convenience we sometimes desperately need in the morning. Quick and easy to prepare, this smoothie is packed with protein, calcium and vitamins C and D. Personalize the recipe by substituting your favourite fruits.

Quinoa flour	1 tbsp.	15 mL
Boiling water	2 tbsp.	30 mL
Chopped mango	1 cup	250 mL
Blackberries	1/2 cup	125 mL
Flaxseed	1 tbsp.	15 mL
Honey	1 tbsp.	15mL
Vanilla extract	1 tsp.	5 mL
Milk	3/4 cup	175 mL
Greek yogurt	1/2 cup	125 mL
Cottage cheese	2 tbsp.	30 mL

Place quinoa flour in a blender and set to a low speed, gradually pouring in boiling water to form a paste.

Add remaining 8 ingredients and pulse until completely combined. Served chilled. Makes 2 servings.

1 serving: 280 Calories; 10 g Total Fat (0.5 g Mono, 1.5 g Poly, 5 g Sat); 25 mg Cholesterol; 39 g Carbohydrate (5 g Fibre, 30 g Sugar); 10 g Protein; 150 mg Sodium

Cinnamon Steel Cut Porridge

A recipe the whole family will love. Nutrient packed with low glycemic carbohydrates, protein and fibre, this porridge will keep you going all morning. Makes a great weekend breakfast, or cook it the evening before and pack it up for a healthy breakfast at work.

Water	2 cups	500 mL
Ground cinnamon	1/2 tsp.	2 mL
Apple juice	1 cup	250 mL
Steel cut oats	1 cup	250 mL
Brown sugar	3 tbsp.	45 mL
Milk	2 tbsp.	30 mL
Greek yogurt	1/2 cup	125 mL
Flaxseed	2 tbsp.	30 mL
Fresh red delicious apples	2	2
Lemon juice	1 tbsp.	15 mL
Chopped almonds	1/4 cup	60 mL

Combine water, cinnamon and apple juice in a medium pot on high. Once liquid has reached a boil, stir in oats. Lower heat and cook for 25 minutes, stirring frequently to prevent burning. Once liquid has been absorbed and oats are soft, remove pot from heat and let rest for 2 minutes.

Mix brown sugar, milk, yogurt and flaxseed in a small bowl.

Chop apples into small cubes and toss with lemon juice. Divide porridge among 4 bowls and spoon yogurt mixture over top. Sprinkle with chopped apple and almonds. Serves 4.

1 serving: 370 Calories; 10 g Total Fat (3 g Mono, 3 g Poly, 3 g Sat); 10 mg Cholesterol; 64 g Carbohydrate (9 g Fibre, 31 g sugar); 9 g Protein; 30 mg Sodium

Dark Chocolate Banana Flapjacks

This recipe uses unique tricks to offer the pleasures of traditional decadent, whipped cream–smothered pancakes with substantially less fat and calories (and therefore less guilt).

All-purpose flour	1 cup	250 mL
Sugar	2 tbsp.	30 mL
Baking powder	1 tsp.	5 mL
Baking soda	1/2 tsp.	2 mL
Salt	1/2 tsp.	2 mL
Chopped dark chocolate	1/3 cup	75 mL
Buttermilk	1/2 cup	125 mL
Milk	1/4 cup	60 mL
Butter, melted	2 tbsp.	30 mL
White vinegar	1 tsp.	5 mL
Egg	1	1
Bananas	2	2
Butter	1 tbsp.	15 mL
Egg whites	4	4
Cream of tartar	1/4 tsp.	1 mL
Sugar	1/4 cup	60 mL
Maple syrup	1/4 cup	60 mL
Agave syrup	1/4 cup	60 mL

Sift together flour, first amount of sugar, baking powder, baking soda and salt in a large mixing bowl, then add dark chocolate. Make a well in centre.

In a separate bowl, whisk together buttermilk, milk, first amount of butter, vinegar and egg. Pour into well in flour mixture and gently whisk until no lumps remain. Do not over mix.

Cut 1 banana in half and set one half aside. Cut remaining banana into thin slices. Melt 1 tsp. (5 mL) butter in a large skillet over medium heat. Pour approximately 1/4 cup (60 mL) batter per pancake onto skillet and top with a few sliced bananas. Cook until bubbles appear on surface, then flip with a spatula and cook until lightly browned on other side. Add butter to pan between batches as needed. Keep warm in 275°F (140°C) oven.

Add egg whites and cream of tartar to bowl of a stand mixer. Whip until soft peaks form, then gradually pour in remaining sugar. Continue to whip until firm peaks form. In a separate bowl, mash banana half, then fold into egg whites. Transfer to a medium bowl and chill in refrigerator until needed.

In a small bowl, mix together maple syrup and agave. To serve, garnish each pancake with a dollop of whipped topping, a drizzle of syrup and some freshly cut bananas. Makes 4 servings.

1 serving: 530 Calories; 16 g Total Fat (3 g Mono, 0.5 g Poly, 9 g Sat); 85 mg Cholesterol; 93 g Carbohydrate (3 g Fibre, 43 g Sugar); 9 g Protein; 670 mg Sodium

Forgiving Egg Bake

Ham and Swiss baked with whole grain bread and a shot of dill. With a little advanced planning, this recipe can be a lifesaver on a busy morning. Slap it together the night before and let it soak overnight, then pop it in the oven the next morning and leave it to work its magic.

Butter	1 tsp.	5 mL
Loaf of whole grain bread	1	1
Cooked ham, diced	1/2 lb.	225 g
Diced green pepper	1 1/2 cups	375 mL
Grated Swiss cheese	3 cups	750 mL
Eggs	8	8
Milk	3 cups	750 mL
Chopped fresh dill	2 tbsp.	30 mL
Hot sauce	1 tsp.	5 mL
Cracked pepper	1/2 tsp.	2 mL
Red wine vinegar	1 tsp.	5 mL

Lightly grease a 9 x 13 inch (23 x 33 cm) casserole with butter. Line bottom of dish with an even layer of bread. You may have to cut bread to fit snugly. For next layer, spread 1/4 lb. (113 g) ham and 3/4 cup (175 mL) green pepper over bread. Repeat sequence, then sprinkle cheese evenly over top.

In a medium bowl, whisk eggs and gradually pour in milk. Add dill, hot sauce, pepper and vinegar. Pour evenly over contents of dish and cover with plastic wrap. Refrigerate for at least 7 hours. To cook, remove plastic wrap and bake in 325°F (160°C) oven for 40 minutes. Remove from oven and let rest for 5 minutes before serving. Makes 8 servings.

1 serving: 410 Calories; 24 g Total Fat (7 g Mono, 1.5 g Poly, 12 g Sat); 280 mg Cholesterol; 27 g Carbohydrate (3 g Fibre; 9 g Sugar); 28 g Protein; 760 mg Sodium

Greek White Omelette

A light, Mediterranean-inspired dish with complete nutrition and a fraction of the fat found in most omelettes.

Egg whites	8	8
Salt	1/8 tsp.	0.5 mL
Pepper	1/8 tsp.	0.5 mL
Cayenne pepper	1/8 tsp.	0.5 mL
Chopped fresh oregano	1/4 tsp.	1 mL
Diced white mushrooms	1/2 cup	125 mL
Butter	1/2 tbsp.	7 mL
Fresh spinach leaves, roughly chopped	1 cup	250 mL
Diced red onion	1/4 cup	60 mL
Butter	1/2 tbsp.	7 mL
Green olives, diced	4	4
Diced tomato	1/4 cup	60 mL
Diced green pepper	1/4 cup	60 mL
Feta cheese, crumbled	3 oz.	85 g

Mix first 5 ingredients together in a small bowl. Set aside.

Heat a medium sized heavy bottomed pot on medium-high and sauté mushrooms in first amount of butter until they begin to brown. Toss in spinach and onion and cook for an additional minute.

Add remaining butter, then pour egg mixture into pan and lower heat. Tip pan from side to side to allow uncooked egg on top to roll to side of pan and cook. Using a rubber spatula, wipe down edges of pan to keep cooked egg loose in pan.

Once bottom of omelette begins to feel firm, flip egg (see Tip, page 29). Mix together olives, tomato, green pepper and half of cheese and sprinkle over half of omelette. Fold omelette in half and cover with remaining cheese. Remove from heat. Cover with a large plate and let rest for 5 minutes before serving. Makes 2 servings.

1 serving: 260 Calories; 16 g Total Fat (3.5 g Mono, 0.5 g Poly, 10 g Sat); 55 mg Cholesterol; 8 g Carbohydrate (1 g Fibre, 5 g Sugar); 20 g Protein; 1090 mg Sodium

Polka Dot Quinoa Omelette

A mildly spicy omelette with red quinoa, Southern seasoned chicken and melted Swiss cheese. This dish is a great breakfast choice for those looking to increase their protein intake.

Large eggs	5	5
Milk	2 tbsp.	30 mL
Chopped fresh oregano	1/2 tsp.	2 mL
Salt	1/4 tsp.	1 mL
Pepper	1/4 tsp.	1 mL
Butter	1/2 tbsp.	7 mL
Diced cooked chicken breast	3/4 cup	175 mL
Diced red pepper	1/2 cup	125 mL
Diced red onion	2 tbsp.	30 mL
Paprika	1 tsp.	5 mL
Cayenne pepper	1/4 tsp.	1 mL
Chipotle chili powder	1/4 tsp.	1 mL
Lemon juice	1 tbsp.	15 mL
Cooked red quinoa	1/4 cup	60 mL
Butter	1/2 tbsp.	7 mL
Cooked red quinoa	1/4 cup	60 mL
Grated Swiss cheese	1/2 cup	125 mL
Hot sauce	1/2 tsp.	2 mL

In a medium bowl, mix first 5 ingredients until combined. Set aside.

Melt first amount of butter in a large heavy bottomed non-stick pan over medium-high. Add chicken, red pepper and onion. Sauté for 1 minute or until onion begins to soften. Mix in paprika, cayenne, chipotle, lemon juice and first amount of quinoa. Lower heat to medium and cook for an additional 2 minutes, stirring frequently. Remove from pan and set aside.

Wipe pan clean with paper towel. Return to high heat and melt remaining butter. Pour in egg mixture and lower heat to medium. Tip pan from side to side to allow uncooked egg on top to roll to side of pan and cook. Use a rubber spatula to wipe down edges of pan to keep cooked egg loose in pan. Sprinkle remaining quinoa evenly over egg. Once bottom of omelette begins to feel firm, flip egg (see Tip).

Turn heat to low and spread chicken mixture over half of omelette. Sprinkle 3/4 cheese over top and cook for a minute or so. Fold in half and sprinkle remaining cheese over top. Remove from heat and allow cheese to melt, then drizzle hot sauce over top before serving. Makes 2 servings.

1 serving: *540 Calories; 31 g Total Fat (10 g Mono, 3 g Poly, 14 g Sat); 613 mg Cholesterol;*
31 g Carbohydrate (3 g Fibre, 4 g Sugar); 35 g Protein; 480 mg Sodium

Tip: If flipping your omelette in the pan means you are at risk of losing your
breakfast to your pooch, try this simple trick. Lay a similar-sized plate or
saucer face down over your omelette and, pushing down on the plate with
one hand, flip the pan over. Wiggle the pan and lift it of the plate. Return
the pan to the stove top and carefully slide the omelette back into the pan.

Peppered Egg Quesadillas

Quesadillas aren't just for dinner anymore! A nutritious and delicious hand-held breakfast that's sure to please the kids.

Whole wheat flour tortillas (9 inch, 23 cm, diameter)	2	2
Grated jalapeño Monterey Jack cheese	2 tbsp.	30 mL
Canola oil	1/2 tsp.	2 mL
Sliced fresh white mushrooms	1/2 cup	125 mL
Chopped red pepper	1/4 cup	60 mL
Eggs, fork-beaten	2	2
Chopped green onion	2 tbsp.	30 mL
Pepper	1/8 tsp.	0.5 mL
Grated jalapeño Monterey Jack cheese	2 tbsp.	30 mL

Place 1 tortilla on an ungreased baking sheet. Sprinkle with first amount of cheese. Set aside.

Heat canola oil in a medium non-stick frying pan on medium. Add mushrooms and red pepper. Cook for about 3 minutes, stirring occasionally, until red pepper is softened.

Add eggs. Sprinkle with green onion and pepper. Reduce heat to medium-low. Cook, covered, for about 2 minutes, without stirring, until eggs are set. Slide egg mixture onto tortilla on baking sheet.

Sprinkle with second amount of cheese. Place remaining tortilla on top. Bake in 400°F (200°C) oven for about 3 minutes until cheese is melted. Cut into wedges. Makes 2 servings.

1 serving: 330 Calories; 18 g Total Fat (8 g Mono, 2 g Poly, 5 g Sat); 225 mg Cholesterol; 30 g Carbohydrate (6 g Fibre, 2 g Sugar); 17 g Protein; 670 mg Sodium

Ultimate Breakfast Sandwich

This hearty sandwich uses the warm yolk of a soft poached egg to sauce the sandwich, resulting in less total fat. A freshly made sandwich can be a healthier, more nutritious alternative to your typical fast food breakfast. It may seem like a big job, but if you're organized, this sandwich can be easily be made in 15 minutes.

Water	2 cups	500 mL
Vinegar	1 tbsp.	15 mL
Eggs	4	4
Bacon strips	4	4
Butter	1 tbsp.	15 mL
Yukon Gold potato, shredded into cold water	1	1
Dried oregano	1/4 tsp.	1 mL
Salt	1/4 tsp.	1 mL
Pepper	1/4 tsp.	1 mL
Cheddar cheese, grated	2 oz.	57 g
Paprika	1/2 tsp.	2 mL
English muffins	4	4
Ketchup	2 tbsp.	30 mL
Head of butter leaf lettuce	1	1

Add water and vinegar to a shallow pot and set on high heat to boil. Once pot of water has reached a boil, lower heat to just below a simmer. Gently crack eggs into water one at time and cook until white is firm but yolk is still soft, about 4 to 5 minutes.

Heat a medium sized heavy bottomed non-stick pan over high. Add bacon strips and lower heat to medium-high. Cook bacon until crispy, pouring out fat as it accumulates. Transfer cooked strips to paper towel and set aside.

Pour out remaining bacon fat and return pan to high heat. Add butter. Drain potatoes and add to hot pan, tossing continuously as they brown. Once potatoes begin to crisp, season with oregano, salt and pepper. Lower heat to medium-high and cover with cheese. Remove from heat and sprinkle with paprika. Let rest for 2 minutes so cheese can melt.

Lightly toast English muffins. Layer sandwiches in following sequence: 1/2 English muffin, ketchup, lettuce, potatoes, egg, bacon, 1/2 English muffin. Give sandwiches a quick little punch to crack the egg yolk. Makes 4 servings.

1 serving: 520 Calories; 31 g Total Fat (10 g Mono, 3 g Poly, 13 g Sat); 260 mg Cholesterol; 43 g Carbohydrate (5 g Fibre, 6 g Sugar); 19 g Protein; 1230 mg Sodium

Tip: The sequence in which you layer the ingredients in this sandwich will have a significant effect on the overall texture and mouth feel. You'll know when you've got it right.

Buffalo Chicken Flatbread

With spicy seasoned chicken, shredded lettuce and ripe tomato, these tasty pitas are a healthier alternative to take-out pizza. They also make a great addition to a school or work lunch bag—just assemble them the night before and grab one on your way out the door in the morning.

Tomato paste	1/2 cup	125 mL
Pineapple juice	2 tbsp.	30 mL
Hot sauce or sriracha	1 tbsp.	15 mL
Cayenne pepper	1/4 tsp.	1 mL
Chopped fresh oregano	1/4 tsp.	1 mL
Canola oil	1 tbsp.	15 mL
Boneless, skinless chicken , cut in 1/2 x 1 inch (12 x 25 mm) strips	1 lb.	454 g
Salt	1/4 tsp.	1 mL
Whole grain pita breads (8 inch, 20 cm, diameter)	4	4
Red onion, halved vertically and sliced 1/16 inch (1.5 mm) thick	1/2	1/2
Roma tomato, diced	1	1
Cheddar cheese, grated	4 oz.	113 g
Head of green leaf lettuce, shredded	1	1
Mayonnaise	3 tbsp.	45 mL
Chipotle chili powder	1/2 tsp.	2 mL

Combine first 5 ingredients and mix until well combined.

Heat oil in a medium sized heavy bottomed pan on medium. Add chicken and cook for 1 minute, then add 1 tbsp. (15 mL) tomato mixture. Add salt and continue to cook until chicken is firm and white throughout. Set aside.

Arrange pita breads on a clear workspace. Spread each shell with tomato mixture, reserving 2 tbsp. (30 mL). Top evenly with onion, tomato, cooked chicken and cheese. Bake in 425°F (220°C) oven for 12 to 15 minutes until hot and crispy. Remove from oven and top with shredded lettuce.

Combine remaining 2 tbsp. (30 mL) tomato mixture with mayonnaise and chipotle and transfer to a squeeze bottle. Top each pizza with a quick drizzle of spicy mayonnaise. Makes 4 servings.

1 serving: 570 Calories; 24 g Total Fat (7 g Mono, 4.5 g Poly, 8 g Sat); 100 mg Cholesterol; 50 g Carbohydrate (10 g Fibre, 8 g Sugar); 43 g Protein; 940 mg Sodium

Caramelized Apple Tempeh

A delicious vegetarian option using tofu's honourable cousin, tempeh, which offers more protein, vitamins and dietary fibre. This sandwich attracts attention with caramelized apple and peppery arugula stacked between toasted rye. Pumpernickel bread would also work well.

Gala apples	3	3
Lemon juice	1 tbsp.	15 mL
Ground cinnamon	1/8 tsp.	0.5 mL
Brown sugar	1 tsp.	5 mL
Butter	1 tsp.	5 mL
Water	2 cups	500 mL
Slices rye or whole grain bread	4	4
Peanut butter	2 tbsp.	30 mL
Arugula	1 cup	250 mL
Tempeh, smoked	8 oz.	225 g
Swiss cheese	2 oz.	57 g

Using a vegetable peeler, peel apple skin and discard, then continue peeling apple down to core, placing slices into a bowl with lemon juice, cinnamon and brown sugar. Heat butter in a heavy bottomed pan over medium-high. Add apples, tossing until they begin to caramelize and pan dries, then add a splash of water a little at a time. Repeat this process until apples are soft and golden brown. Set aside.

Gently toast rye bread and place on a clean work surface. Arrange sandwich in the following sequence: bread, peanut butter, arugula, tempeh, cheese, apples, bread. Cut each sandwich diagonally and serve warm. Makes 2 servings.

1 serving: 780 Calories; 29 g Total Fat (1.5 g Mono, 1 g Poly, 10 g Sat); 30 mg Cholesterol; 97 g Carbohydrate (15 g Fibre, 38 g Sugar); 41 g Protein; 690 mg Sodium

Crab and Mango Salad Rolls

Soft crab, cool cucumber and sweet mango rolled into a tasty snack. Adding an ice cube to the sauce mellows it out and cools it down quickly, so you don't have to wait to dig in.

Rice wine vinegar	2 tbsp.	30 mL
Fish sauce	2 tbsp.	30 mL
Lemon juice	1 tsp.	5 mL
Agave syrup	1 tsp.	5 mL
Peel of carrot, about 2 inches (5 cm) long	1	1
Peel of ginger root, about 2 inches (5 cm) long	1	1
Small ice cube	1	1
Sheets of rice paper (8 inch, 20 cm, diameter)	8	8
Vermicelli, cooked	1 cup	250 mL
Crab leg meat	8 oz.	225 g
Cucumber, julienned	1/2	1/2
Carrot, julienned	1/2	1/2
Mango, cut into thin strips	1	1
Red pepper, julienned	1/2	1/2
Black sesame seeds	1 tbsp.	15 mL

Combine vinegar, fish sauce, lemon juice and agave in a small bowl. Add thin peel of carrot and ginger root and microwave for 45 seconds or until hot to the touch. Stir in ice cube and set aside.

Fill a shallow pan with warm water. Soak rice paper, one sheet at a time, for 45 seconds. Remove from water and place on a clean work surface. Layer in vermicelli, crab, cucumber, carrot, mango and red pepper. Roll tightly and tuck edges into centre. Repeat with remaining sheets. Roll half of roll in black sesame seeds and slice in half on a bias. Serve chilled with cooled sauce. Makes 4 servings.

1 serving: 200 Calories; 2 g Total Fat (0.5 g Mono, 0.5 g Poly, 0 g Sat); 25 mg Cholesterol; 32 g Carbohydrate (3 g Fibre, 8 g Sugar); 13 g Protein; 1170 mg Sodium

Tip: It may be helpful to place a clean, damp towel under the sheets of rice paper while you are rolling them to prevent sticking. It is also a good idea to cover completed rolls with moist paper towel to prevent them from drying out as you are working on others.

Cranberry and Turkey Sandwich

Flavours that pair so well together, it's a delight to see them snug inside a sandwich. This recipe is also a great way to use up turkey leftovers. For the best results, slice the ingredients for this sandwich thin and layer them in sequence. It makes for a real balance in flavour and texture.

Chopped dried cranberries	2 tbsp.	30 mL
Water	1 tbsp.	15 mL
Lemon juice	1 tsp.	5 mL
Mayonnaise	2 tbsp.	30 mL
Prepared mustard	1 tsp.	5 mL
Slices whole grain or rye bread	4	4
Baked turkey breast, thinly sliced	6 oz.	170 g
Small cucumber, sliced thinly on a bias	1	1
Cheddar cheese, thinly sliced (see Tip)	3 oz.	85 g
Bundle of watercress, stems trimmed	1	1

Place cranberries, water and lemon juice in a small bowl and microwave for 45 seconds. Let rest for 2 minutes, then mix in mayonnaise and mustard.

Lightly toast bread and generously spread with cranberry mayonnaise. Layer turkey, cucumber, cheese and watercress between 2 bread slices. Cut in half diagonally. Serve warm. Makes 2 servings.

1 serving: 600 Calories; 29 g Total Fat (8 g Mono, 4.5 g Poly, 11 g Sat); 85 mg Cholesterol; 45 g Carbohydrate (5 g Fibre, 8 g Sugar) 36 g Protein; 1180 mg Sodium

Tip: Is slicing cheese thinly a real challenge for you? Try using your vegetable peeler—it can give you a perfect, stress-free result.

Egg Salad Panini

The key to this sandwich is to cook the eggs until the yolks have a gel-like consistency, which then holds all the other ingredients together without the need for added fat.

Eggs	8	8
Lemon juice	1 tbsp.	15 mL
Mayonnaise	1 tbsp.	15 mL
Chopped fresh dill	1/2 tsp.	2 mL
Chopped fresh sage	1/2 tsp.	2 mL
Garlic clove, minced	1	1
Grainy Dijon mustard	1 tbsp.	15 mL
Worcestershire sauce	1/4 tsp.	1 mL
Cayenne pepper	1/8 tsp.	0.5 mL
Chipotle chili powder	1/8 tsp.	0.5 mL
Salt	1/8 tsp.	0.5 mL
Pepper	1/8 tsp.	0.5 mL
Flaxseed	1 tsp.	5 mL
Radishes, thinly sliced	4	4
Whole grain pita breads	4	4
Hummus	1/3 cup	75 mL
Head of leaf lettuce, shredded	1	1
Provolone cheese, grated	6 oz.	170 g

Place eggs in a medium pot filled with cool water. Place pot over high heat and bring to a boil. Lower heat and simmer for about 3 minutes—eggs yolks should still be soft. Remove eggs from water and chill in ice water. Remove shells. Using a grater, shred eggs into a medium sized bowl and gently fold in next 13 ingredients. Set aside.

Lay pita breads flat on counter and cover half of each with hummus. Next, layer with shredded lettuce. Spoon egg salad mixture generously over top and finish with cheese. Tightly roll each pita. Set on a hot grill press for 1 minute on each side, until lightly crisp and marked. Makes 4 servings.

1 serving: 540 Calories; 27 g Total Fat (9 g Mono, 3.5 g Poly, 11 g Sat); 450 mg Cholesterol; 52 g Carbohydrate (9 g Fibre, 3 g Sugar); 27 g Protein; 1077 mg Sodium

Tip: The true quality of this recipe lies in the lightness of the egg mixture, so be sure to use a gentle hand when combining the ingredients.

Broccoli Bacon Cheddar Soup

This family favourite is high in vitamin C and calcium, making it great for the immune system. Comfort food at its best!

Pork or vegetable stock	4 cups	1 L
Milk	2 cups	500 mL
Butter	2 tbsp.	30 mL
All-purpose flour	3 tbsp.	45 mL
Bacon slices	6	6
White onion, diced	1	1
Heads of broccoli, cut into small florets	2	2
Cheddar cheese, grated	5 oz.	140 g
Lemon juice	2 tbsp.	30 mL
Salt	3/4 tsp.	4 mL
Pepper	1/2 tsp.	2 mL
Ground fennel seed	1/4 tsp.	1 mL
Chopped fresh parsley	1/4 cup	60 mL

In a medium sized pot mix together stock and milk and bring to a boil. Melt butter in a large heavy bottomed pot over medium heat. Stir in flour to make a paste. Gradually add stock mixture, one ladle at a time, and whisk until well combined before adding another ladle. Once all liquid has been added, lower heat and simmer for 20 minutes.

Cook bacon in a heavy bottomed pan over medium-high heat until crisp, pouring out fat as it accumulates. Remove cooked bacon and set aside. Reserving about 2 tbsp. (30 mL) of fat in pan, lower heat and gently cook onion and broccoli for 4 minutes, then add to thickened liquid.

Increase heat to medium and fold in cheese, lemon juice, salt, pepper and fennel. Simmer for 5 minutes.

Chop bacon into large chunks. Stir bacon and chopped parsley into soup, and serve. Makes 6 servings.

1 serving: 370 Calories; 30 g Total Fat (9 g Mono, 2 g Poly, 14 g Sat); 70 mg Cholesterol; 12 g Carbohydrate (trace Fibre, 6 g Sugar); 14 g Protein; 840 mg Sodium

Lentil Tofu Soup

This full-bodied soup pairs green lentils and tofu with the sweetness of mango. A great source of folate, iron, vitamin B12 and dietary fibre, this soup also provides complete protein. A perfect vegan choice!

Green lentils	3/4 cup	175 mL
Vegetable stock	10 cups	2.5 L
Rice wine vinegar	1 tbsp.	15 mL
Low-sodium soy sauce	2 tbsp.	30 mL
Bay leaves	2	2
Curry powder	3/4 tsp.	4 mL
White onion, sliced 1/8 inch (3 mm) thick	1	1
Diced dried mango	1/2 cup	125 mL
Napa cabbage, cut into 1 inch (2.5 cm) squares	2 cups	500 mL
Diced firm tofu	1 1/2 cups	375 mL
Enoki mushrooms	1 cup	250 mL
Green onions, thinly sliced on a bias	2	2
Sesame seeds	2 tbsp.	30 mL
Nutritional yeast	2 tbsp.	30 mL

Combine first 6 ingredients in a large pot and bring to a boil. Lower heat and add onion and dried mango. Simmer for 30 minutes or until lentils are cooked. Discard bay leaves and fold in cabbage and tofu. Continue to simmer for another 5 minutes.

Remove from heat and gently mix in enoki mushrooms, green onion, sesame seeds and nutritional yeast. Let rest for 10 minutes to infuse flavours. Makes 6 servings.

1 serving: 220 Calories; 4.5 g Total Fat (1.5 g Mono, 1.5 g Poly, 0.5 g Sat); 0 mg Cholesterol; 32 g Carbohydrate (7 g Fibre, 10 g Sugar); 14 g Protein; 220 mg Sodium

Tip: Be sure to let this soup rest after it has been cooked so that the tofu has time to be infused with the soup's rich flavours. The end result is well worth the wait.

Sham Sou'

A quality time saver for all those who appreciate a good short cut, this recipe transforms a canned soup into a nutritious, delicious meal. Augmenting a canned soup with vegetables, fresh herbs and stock also reduces its sodium content per serving.

Dried mushrooms (such as chanterelle, morel or portobello)	1 cup	250 mL
Butter	1 tbsp.	15 mL
Diced onion	1/4 cup	60 mL
Diced celery	1/4 cup	60 mL
Chopped fresh rosemary	1/4 tsp.	1 mL
10 oz. (284 mL) can of condensed cream of mushroom soup	1	1
Milk	1 1/2 cup	375 mL
Cheddar cheese, grated	1 oz.	28 g
Lemon juice	1 tsp.	5 mL
Cracked pepper	1/4 tsp.	1 mL

Place mushrooms in a tall, narrow glass and add boiling water to cover, weighing the mushrooms down with a smaller glass. Let rehydrate for 10 minutes. Remove from water and reserve liquid. Transfer to a cutting board and chop. Set aside.

Melt butter in a large heavy bottomed pan over medium-high heat. Toss in onion, celery and rosemary and sauté until onions begin to sweat. Adjust heat to high and add chopped mushrooms and 1 cup (250 mL) of mushroom liquid. Cook until reduced by three-quarters.

Add canned soup and milk, whisking until well mixed. Fold in cheese. Adjust seasoning with lemon juice and cracked pepper. Let rest for 2 minutes before serving. Makes 4 servings.

1 serving: 170 Calories; 9 g Total Fat (1.5 g Mono, 0.5 g Poly, 5 g Sat); 30 mg Cholesterol; 15 g Carbohydrate (0 g Fibre, 7 g Sugar); 7 g Protein; 680 mg Sodium

Tip: You can expand upon this versatile recipe by using some of your favourite soups and vegetables.

Soba Chicken Soup

In this take on chicken noodle soup, a comforting classic is revamped with the addition of buckwheat noodles and a pinch of ginger. Loaded with vitamins and minerals, this soup helps boost the immune system.

Olive oil	1 tbsp.	15 mL
White onion, diced	1	1
Ribs of celery, diced	2	2
Carrot, shredded	1	1
Boneless, skinless chicken breast, diced	1 lb.	454 g
Garlic cloves, minced	2	2
Minced ginger root	1 tsp.	5 mL
Low-sodium soy sauce	3 tbsp.	45 mL
Ground cumin	1/4 tsp.	1 mL
Cayenne pepper	1/8 tsp.	0.5 mL
Cornstarch	2 tbsp.	30 mL
Chicken or vegetable stock, or water	6 cups	1.5 L
Chickpeas	3/4 cup	175 mL
Soba noodles	3 1/2 oz.	100 g
Chopped fresh parsley	1/4 cup	60 mL

Heat oil in a heavy bottomed pot over medium-high. Add onion, celery and carrot and cook until vegetables begin to sweat. Add chicken, garlic, ginger root, soy sauce, cumin and cayenne. Lower heat to medium and cook for another 4 minutes.

Sprinkle cornstarch evenly over top, then gradually pour stock into pot, whisking continuously. Bring to a boil, then lower heat to a simmer. Stir in chickpeas and soba noodles and simmer until noodles are tender, about 3 to 4 minutes. Add parsley and serve. Makes 8 servings.

1 serving: 180 Calories; 3 g Total Fat (1.5 g Mono, 0 g Poly, 0 g Sat); 35 mg Cholesterol; 21 g Carbohydrate (3 g Fibre, 2 g Sugar); 17 g Protein; 330 mg Sodium

Tip: Serve this soup as soon as it has finished cooking. Soba noodles are very fine and delicate, and if they sit in a hot liquid for a long time, they may become soggy and unpleasant.

Wild Mushroom Broth

A simple yet defined soup that truly captures the essence of mushrooms with a subtle touch of white onion. Pairs well with a beefy sandwich for a great lunch.

Dried mushrooms (such as chanterelle, morel or portobello)	2 cups	500 mL
Boiling water	6 cups	1.5 L
Butter	1 tbsp.	15 mL
White onion, cut into 1/8 inch (3 mm) slices	1/2	1/2
Agave syrup	1 tbsp.	15 mL
Red wine vinegar	1 tbsp.	15 mL
Sprig of rosemary	1	1
Bay leaf	1	1

Place mushrooms in a large bowl and cover with boiling water, weighing the mushrooms down with a large plate to fully submerge. Soak for 10 minutes.

Meanwhile, melt butter in a large heavy bottomed pot over medium-high. Add onions and cook until they sweat without browning, about 3 minutes. Lower heat and mix in agave, vinegar, rosemary and bay leaf. Drain mushrooms by pouring liquid into pot. Transfer mushrooms to a cutting board and chop roughly. Add chopped mushrooms to pot and simmer for 20 minutes. Discard rosemary and bay leaf and serve. Makes 6 servings.

1 serving: 45 Calories; 2 g Total Fat (0 g Mono, 0 g Poly, 1 g Sat); 5 mg Cholesterol; 8 g Carbohydrate (0 g Fibre, 1 g Sugar); 0 g Protein; 15 mg Sodium

Black Bean Bolognaise

A comfort meat sauce that is high protein and fibre. Use it for sloppy Joes or as a hearty accompaniment for pasta, rice or potatoes (as shown in the photo). For a little variety, substitute chickpeas or kidney beans for the black beans.

Extra-lean ground beef	1 lb.	454 g
Diced white onion	1/3 cup	75 mL
Diced celery	1/3 cup	75 mL
Diced carrot	1/3 cup	75 mL
Diced white mushrooms	1/2 cup	125 mL
Butter	1 tbsp.	15 mL
Red wine or water	1/2 cup	125 mL
Green olives, finely chopped	8	8
Tomato sauce	1/2 cup	125 mL
Finely chopped rosemary	1/4 tsp.	1 mL
Dijon (or prepared) mustard	1 tbsp.	15 mL
Milk	1/2 cup	125 mL
Cooked black beans	1 cup	250 mL
Salt	1/2 tsp.	2 mL
Pepper	1/2 tsp.	2 mL
Brown sugar	1 tbsp.	15 mL
Lemon, juiced	1	1
Paprika	1 tsp.	5 mL
Cayenne pepper	1/2 tsp.	2 mL

Heat a large pan over high. Add ground beef, breaking it up with a spatula, and cook until brown. Drain fat, then add onion, celery, carrot, mushrooms and butter. Continue to cook on high heat until vegetables begin to soften and brown.

Add red wine, shake pan and lower heat to medium. Mix in remaining ingredients. Simmer on low to medium heat for 10 minutes until thickened. Remove from heat and serve. Makes 6 servings.

1 serving: 230 Calories; 7 g Total Fat (2.5 g Mono, 0 g Poly, 3 g Sat); 55 mg Cholesterol; 16 g Carbohydrate (3 g Fibre, 6 g Sugar); 21 g Protein; 550 mg Sodium

Crispy Mac 'n' Cheese

Classic beefy macaroni and cheese with the added nutrition of carrot and quinoa. Your kids will lick their plates clean.

Vegetable stock or water	1 L	4 cups
Red quinoa, rinsed	1/2 cup	125 mL
Salt	1/4 tsp.	1 mL
Elbow macaroni	3 cups	750 mL
Extra-lean ground beef	1/2 lb.	225 g
Diced carrot	1 cup	250 mL
All-purpose flour	1 tbsp.	15 mL
Milk	1 3/4 cups	425 mL
Monterey Jack cheese, grated	6 oz.	170 g
Ground nutmeg	1/8 tsp.	0.5 mL
Salt	1/4 tsp.	1 mL
Lemon juice	1 tbsp.	15 mL
Cheddar cheese, grated	5 oz.	140 g
Whole grain bread crumbs or panko	1/2 cup	125 mL

Bring vegetable stock to a boil in a large pot. Stir in quinoa and first amount of salt and cook for 5 minutes before stirring in macaroni. Cover with lid and cook for an additional 7 minutes. When finished, liquid should all be absorbed. Transfer to a large bowl and set aside.

Cook ground beef in a large heavy bottomed pan over high until browned. Add carrot and lower heat, cooking for an additional 4 minutes. Transfer to bowl with pasta. Add flour to pan and gradually whisk in milk until well combined. Adjust heat to medium and allow sauce to heat and thicken. Once sauce has reached a boil, lower heat and stir in Monterey Jack, nutmeg, remaining salt and lemon juice. Simmer for another 5 minutes.

Combine sauce, pasta and ground beef in a large bowl. Mix well. Pour mixture into a 9 x 13 inch (23 x 33 cm) baking dish. Combine Cheddar cheese and bread crumbs and sprinkle over top. Bake in 400°F (200°C) oven for 10 minutes, then broil until crispy and golden brown, about 3 minutes. Let rest for 4 minutes before serving. Makes 6 servings.

1 serving: 570 Calories; 21 g Total Fat (1 g Mono, 0 g Poly, 12 g Sat); 80 mg Cholesterol; 62 g Carbohydrate (3 g Fibre, 7 g Sugar); 34 g Protein; 660 mg Sodium

Tip: For a creamier result, add up to 1/4 cup (60 mL) of water. You may need to add more water if you are using whole grain pasta.

Rocket Red Burgers

Roasted red pepper and arugula give these hearty mini burgers a little spark. Homemade burgers provide better nutrition than your average fast food burger because they use fresher ingredients and contain much less saturated fat and sodium.

Extra-lean ground beef	1 3/4 lbs.	790 g
Diced red onion	1/2 cup	125 mL
Garlic cloves, finely diced	4	4
Eggs	2	2
Bread crumbs	1/2 cup	125 mL
Chopped Italian parsley	1/4 cup	60 mL
Salt	1/4 tsp.	1 mL
Pepper	1/2 tsp.	2 mL
Paprika	1 tbsp.	15 mL
Low-sodium soy sauce	1 tbsp.	15 mL
Chopped fresh thyme	1/4 tsp.	1 mL
Roasted red peppers	1/2 cup	125 mL
Garlic clove	1	1
Lemon juice	1 tsp.	5 mL
Chipotle chili powder	1/8 tsp.	0.5 mL
Paprika	1/4 tsp.	1 mL
Light mayonnaise	1/2 cup	125 mL
Prepared mustard	1 tbsp.	15 mL
Whole mozzarella, sliced into 12 pieces	6 oz.	170 g
Mini Ciabatta buns	12	12
Arugula, lightly packed	2 cups	500 mL
Roma (plum) tomatoes, thinly sliced	3	3
Red onion, thinly sliced	1	1

Mix the first 11 ingredients together in a medium sized bowl then press into 3 oz. (85 g) balls—slightly larger than the size of a golf ball. Place on a baking sheet lined with parchment paper and let rest in refrigerator for 20 minutes.

Blend roasted red peppers and mix with garlic, lemon juice, chipotle, paprika, mayonnaise and mustard. Set aside.

Flatten each burger with your palm until it is 3/4 inch (2 cm) thick and 3 inches (7.5 cm) in diameter. Bake in 400°F (200°C) oven for 10 minutes, then flip each burger and return to oven. Increase heat to 475°F (240°C) and bake for an additional 10 minutes. Remove from oven, place 1 slice of mozzarella over top and let rest for 5 minutes.

Lightly toast ciabatta buns. Assemble burgers with sauce, tomato, arugula and onion. Makes 6 serving.

1 serving (2 burgers): 560 Calories; 24 g Total Fat (8 g Mono, 5 g Poly, 9 g Sat); 185 mg Cholesterol; 41 g Carbohydrate (3 g Fibre, 5 g Sugar); 43 g Protein; 750 mg Sodium

Tamale Pie

Barley is a unique addition to this low-fat, cornmeal-topped remake of Tamale Pie. You can cook a large batch of barley and then freeze it, and then you'll have some on hand to throw into soups, stews or salads.

Water	8 cups	2 L
Salt	1 tsp.	5 mL
Pot barley	1/3 cup	75 mL
Canola oil	1 tsp.	5 mL
Chopped green pepper	1 cup	250 mL
Chopped onion	1 cup	250 mL
Garlic cloves, minced	2	2
19 oz. (540 mL) can of kidney beans, rinsed and drained	1	1
Chopped tomato	1 1/2 cups	375 mL
Frozen kernel corn	1 cup	250 mL
Chili powder	2 tbsp.	30 mL
Dried crushed chilies	1/2 tsp.	2 mL
Salt	1/4 tsp.	1 mL
Water	3 cups	750 mL
Yellow cornmeal	1 cup	250 mL
Grated jalapeño Monterey Jack cheese	1/2 cup	125 mL
Salsa	1/4 cup	60 mL

Combine first amount of water and salt in a large saucepan. Bring to a boil. Add barley. Reduce heat to medium and boil gently, partially covered, for about 35 minutes, stirring occasionally, until tender. Drain.

Heat canola oil in a large frying pan on medium. Add next 3 ingredients. Cook for about 5 minutes, stirring occasionally, until onion is softened. Stir in next 6 ingredients and barley. Transfer to ungreased 8 x 8 inch (20 x 20 cm) baking dish.

Bring second amount of water to a boil in a medium saucepan. Add cornmeal. Heat, stirring, for about 5 minutes until mixture thickens and pulls away from side of pan. Stir in cheese and salsa. Pour evenly over barley mixture. Bake in 375°F (190°C) oven for about 35 minutes until heated through and topping is set. Makes 6 servings.

1 serving: 288 Calories; 4 g Total Fat (0.5 g Mono, 0 g Poly, 2 g Sat); 9 mg Cholesterol; 51 g Carbohydrate (8 g Fibre, 6 g Sugar); 10 g Protein; 406 mg Sodium

Souvlaki Skewers

Succulent little skewers, marinated in fruit juices, evoke images of a rustic seaside Mediterranean table set for friends, with the lively strains of Greek music in the background. Opa!

Egg, fork-beaten	1	1
Fine dry bread crumbs	1/3 cup	75 mL
Finely chopped onion	1/3 cup	75 mL
Dried oregano	1 tsp.	5 mL
Grated lemon zest	1 tsp.	5 mL
Garlic clove, minced	1	1
Salt	3/4 tsp.	4 mL
Pepper	1/4 tsp.	1 mL
Ground allspice	1/4 tsp.	1 mL
Lean ground beef	1 lb.	454 g
Metal skewers (8 inches, 20 cm, each)	6	6
Apple juice	1/4 cup	60 mL
Lemon juice	3 tbsp.	45 mL
Cooking oil	2 tbsp.	30 mL
Dried oregano	2 tsp.	10 mL
Garlic clove, minced	1	1
Pepper	1/4 tsp.	1 mL

Combine first 10 ingredients and divide into 6 equal portions. Form each portion into a sausage shape, about 6 inches (15 cm) long, and insert skewers.

Combine remaining 6 ingredients in a shallow baking disk. Add skewers, cover and chill for at least 6 hours or overnight, turning occasionally. Drain and discard marinade. Grill skewers on direct medium heat for about 15 minutes, turning often, until internal temperature reaches 160°F (71°C). Makes 6 skewers.

1 skewer: 234 Calories; 15.0 g Total Fat (7.1 g Mono, 1.5 g Poly, 4.7 g Sat); 76 mg Cholesterol; 7 g Carbohydrate (1 g Fibre, 2 g Sugar); 17 g Protein; 403 mg Sodium

Sirloin Roast with Cipollini Onions and Horseradish Cream

This dish is all about the marinade, which helps tenderize the meat as it adds its distinctive flavour. The longer the meat sits in the marinade, the better it will be, so plan ahead. If you cannot find cipollini onions, use pearl onions instead. They work just as well.

Salt	1 tsp.	5 mL
Pepper	1 tsp.	5 mL
Sprigs of fresh rosemary	2	2
Garlic cloves, halved	8	8
Large tomato, diced	1	1
Prepared mustard	2 tbsp.	30 mL
Paprika	1 tsp.	5 mL
Beef top sirloin roast, trimmed of fat	3 lbs.	1.4 kg
Butter	1 tbsp.	15 mL
Cipollini onions, peeled	20	20
White balsamic vinegar	1/4 cup	60 mL
Sour cream	3/4 cup	175 mL
Horseradish	2 tbsp.	30 mL
Green onion, thinly sliced	1	1
Cracked pepper	1/2 tsp.	2 mL

In a large resealable bag combine first 7 ingredients. Add sirloin roast to bag and seal as airtight as possible. Marinate for at least 4 hours.

Melt butter in a heavy bottomed pan over medium heat. Remove roast from bag, reserving marinade, and place in hot pan with cipollini onions. Remove any pieces of garlic or rosemary that may have fallen into pan. Sear each side of roast to a golden brown, then pour vinegar into pan and cook until almost completely evaporated. Place roast fat side up in a roast pan with a wire rack to allow air circulation. Pour 1/4 marinade over meat and top with rosemary and garlic. Bake in 325°F (160°C) oven for 4 hours, returning to baste with marinade every 45 minutes. Cook for an additional hour if you prefer meat to be more well done. Remove from oven, cover and let rest for 10 minutes.

Combine sour cream, horseradish, green onion and cracked pepper in a small bowl. Slice meat into thin strips and serve with a dob of horseradish cream and a few cipollini onions. Makes 6 servings.

1 serving: 610 Calories; 28 g Total Fat (11 g Mono, 1 g Poly, 13 g Sat); 130 mg Cholesterol; 13 g Carbohydrate (1 g Fibre, 2 g Sugar); 45 g Protein; 840 mg Sodium

Tip: Searing before baking can add significant flavour and visual appeal to any meat. For this roast, remove any pieces of garlic or rosemary that may fall into pan while searing or they can burn and give your roast a bitter, unpleasant taste.

Bulgogi Beef

Bring a taste of Korea to your table with this tender, marinated beef. This dish will outshine anything you find on a take-out menu. Serve with hot rice and garnish with green onions and sesame seeds.

Sugar	1/4 cup	60 mL
Mirin	1/4 cup	60 mL
Sesame oil	1/4 cup	60 mL
Soy sauce	1/4 cup	60 mL
Chopped green onion (white part only)	2 tbsp.	30 mL
Garlic cloves, minced	4	4
Finely grated ginger root	2 tsp.	10 mL
Pepper	1/2 tsp.	2 mL
Beef rib-eye steak (1 inch, 2.5 cm, thick), thinly sliced	1 1/2 lbs.	680 g
Cornstarch	1 tsp.	5 mL
Cooking oil	1 tbsp.	15 mL

Combine first 8 ingredients in a large resealable freezer bag. Add beef and marinate in the refrigerator for 2 hours.

Drain marinade into a small cup. Stir in cornstarch until smooth and set aside.

Heat a wok or large frying pan on medium-high. Add cooking oil. Add beef and stir-fry for 2 minutes until browned. Transfer to a bowl and set aside. Stir reserved marinade and add to wok. Stir for 1 minute until bubbling and thickened. Return beef to wok and stir until coated. Makes about 4 cups (1 L).

1/2 cup (125 mL): 260 Calories; 14 g Total Fat (6 g Mono, 3.5 g Poly, 3.5 g Sat); 40 mg Cholesterol; 12 g Carbohydrate (trace Fibre, 11 g Sugar); 18 g Protein; 520 mg Sodium

Braised Borscht Kabobs

A tasty reconstruction of a classic, with more tender pork than you can shake a stick at.

Butter	1 tbsp.	15 mL
Pork loin, cut into 1 inch (2.5 cm) cubes	2 lbs.	900 g
White wine	1 cup	250 mL
Apple juice	2 cups	500 mL
Water	2 cups	500 mL
Red cabbage, quartered, inner leaves removed	1/2	1/2
Ground cinnamon	1/2 tsp.	2 mL
Fennel seed	1/4 tsp.	1 mL
Ground cloves	1/4 tsp.	1 mL
Lemon juice	2 tbsp.	30 mL
Salt	1/2 tsp.	2 mL
Red beets, cut in 1 inch (2.5 cm) chunks	4	4
Leeks (whites only), cut into 1 inch (2.5 cm) chunks	5	5
Carrots, cut into 1 inch (2.5 cm) chunks	5	5
Metal skewers (8 inches, 20 cm, each)	10	10
Sour cream	1/4 cup	60 mL
Chopped dill	2 tsp.	10 mL

Melt butter in a large heavy bottomed, oven-safe pan over medium-high heat. Add pork and sear until golden brown on all sides.

Pour in half white wine to deglaze pan, then add remaining wine, apple juice and water. Break apart cabbage leaves and add to pan. Mix in next 8 ingredients, ensuring meat and vegetables are submerged in liquid. Add more water if necessary. Cook in 350°F (175°C) oven for 2 hours, or until pork chunks can be cut with a fork.

Remove pan from oven and let rest for 15 minutes. Strain liquid into a heavy bottomed pot and cook on high heat until volume is reduced by three-quarters and liquid has reached a syrupy consistency. Adjust oven heat to 450°F (230°C). Thread pork and vegetables evenly on skewers. Generously brush kabobs with syrupy liquid and return to oven to glaze for 5 minutes. Remove from oven and let rest for 4 minutes.

Combine sour cream and dill and transfer to a fine-tip squeeze bottle (see Tip). Squeeze sour cream mixture over top of each kabob and serve. Makes 10 skewers.

1 skewer: 270 Calories; 8 g Total Fat (3 g Mono, 1 g Poly, 3.5 g Sat); 65 mg Cholesterol; 25 g Carbohydrate (4 g Fibre, 14 g Sugar); 21 g Protein; 260 mg Sodium

Tip: If you don't have a squeeze bottle, there are many ways you can improvise. Try poking a small hole in a resealable freezer bag, or use an empty, well-rinsed mustard bottle.

Pulled Pork Quesadillas

All the flavour of a pulled pork sandwich with the added zip and fun-to-eat presentation of a quesadilla. Super kid-friendly! For a little added visual appeal, garnish with a fresh jalapeño slice.

Butter	1 tbsp.	15 mL
Bone-in pork shoulder, trimmed of fat and cut into 2 inch (5 cm) cubes	1	1
12 oz. (355 mL) can of Dr. Pepper soda	1	1
Orange, quartered	1	1
Ground cinnamon	1/4 tsp.	1 mL
Tomato paste	1/2 cup	125 mL
Ground cloves	1/4 tsp.	1 mL
Bay leaves	2	2
Water	3 cups	750 mL
Salt	1/2 tsp.	2 mL
Cracked pepper	1/4 tsp.	1 mL
Butter	1 tbsp.	15 mL
Diced red onion	1/2 cup	125 mL
Diced red pepper	1/2 cup	125 mL
Finely chopped fresh jalapeño pepper	1/4 cup	60 mL
Chopped pineapple	1/4 cup	60 mL
Whole grain tortillas (12 inch, 30 cm, diameter)	6	6
Cheddar cheese, grated	6 oz.	170 g
Chopped arugula	1 cup	250 mL

Melt first amount of butter in a large heavy bottomed pan over medium-high and sear pork until golden brown on all sides. Transfer to a large pot with next 9 ingredients. Bring to a boil, then reduce heat to a simmer. Simmer until pork will tear with a fork, about 3 hours. Once pork is cooked, allow it to cool in cooking liquid for 30 minutes.

Remove pork from liquid and shred by hand until loose. Pour some cooking liquid over top and set aside. Pour remaining liquid into a separate bowl. Return pan to stove and melt remaining butter over medium-high heat. Add onion and cook for 1 minute, then add red pepper, jalapeño and pineapple, cooking for an additional 3 minutes or until onions begin to soften. Fold in pork and 1/2 cup (125 mL) cooking liquid. Cook until liquid has evaporated. Set pan aside to rest for 5 minutes.

Arrange 3 tortillas flat on a work surface and spoon pork mixture equally over top. Sprinkle each with cheese and arugula, and cover with remaining tortillas. Place under hot grill press for 1 1/2 minutes on each side, or until toasted and crispy. Let rest for 2 minutes, then cut each tortilla diagonally into 6 equal pieces. Pairs well with light sour cream and salsa. Makes 6 servings.

1 serving: 380 Calories; 20 g Total Fat (6 g Mono, 1 g Poly, 9 g Sat); 40 mg Cholesterol; 43 g Carbohydrate (8 g Fibre, 12 g Sugar); 14 g Protein; 970 mg Sodium

Ginger Pork

If you love the taste of ginger, this dish is for you! The slight heat from the cayenne pepper will linger in your mouth. Serve with rice noodles.

Sesame (or cooking) oil	2 tbsp.	30 mL
Cornstarch	1/4 cup	60 mL
Boneless pork loin, cut julienne	1 lb.	454 g
Cayenne pepper	1/4 tsp.	1 mL
Cooking oil	1 tbsp.	15 mL
Medium carrots, cut julienne	2	2
Finely chopped peeled ginger root	2 tbsp.	30 mL
Medium onion, cut lengthwise into slivers	1	1
Cooking oil	1 tbsp.	15 mL
Fish sauce	3 tbsp.	45 mL
Indonesian sweet (or thick) soy sauce	2 tbsp.	30 mL
Chopped fresh cilantro (or fresh parsley), for garnish		
Sliced green onion, for garnish		

Stir sesame oil into cornstarch in a medium bowl. Add pork and cayenne pepper. Stir until pork is coated. Let rest for 15 minutes.

Heat wok or large frying pan on medium-high. Add first amount of cooking oil. Add carrot, ginger root and onion. Stir-fry for about 5 minutes until golden. Transfer to bowl.

Add second amount of cooking oil to hot wok. Add pork mixture. Stir-fry for about 3 minutes, keeping pork pieces separate, until browned and no longer pink inside. Stir in carrot mixture. Add fish sauce and soy sauce. Stir-fry for about 1 minute until pork is coated. Sprinkle with cilantro and green onion. Makes 4 servings.

1 serving: 340 Calories; 18.1 g Total Fat (8.7 g Mono, 5.4 g Poly, 2.9 g Sat); 78 mg Cholesterol; 16 g Carbohydrate (2 g Fibre, 11 g Sugar); 27 g Protein; 1668 mg Sodium

Pomme Polenta Pork Loin

Cinnamon-rubbed pork loin stuffed with apple-infused polenta and spinach. Tasty and nutritious, this recipe is sure to have the whole family coming back for seconds.

Pork loin, trimmed of excess fat	2 1/2 lbs.	1.1 kg
Ground cinnamon	1/2 tsp.	2 mL
Chopped fresh sage	1/2 tsp.	2 mL
Salt	1/4 tsp.	1 mL
Pepper	1/2 tsp.	2 mL
Butter	1 tbsp.	15 mL
Shallots, diced	2	2
Garlic cloves, minced	2	2
Green apple, diced	1	1
Chopped fresh parsley	1 tbsp.	15 mL
Red wine vinegar	1 tsp.	5 mL
Salt	1/8 tsp.	0.5 mL
Pork stock or water	1 1/4 cups	300 mL
Cornmeal	3/4 cup	175 mL
Parmesan cheese, grated	2 oz.	57 g
Fresh spinach leaves, lightly packed	4 cups	1 L
White wine, such as Chardonnay	1/2 cup	125 mL
Butter	1 tbsp.	15 mL
Dijon mustard	1 tsp.	5 mL

Place roast fat side up on a cutting board and cut horizontally, about 1 inch (2.5 cm) from bottom, almost but not quite through to other side. Open roast like a book and cut through thicker half of roast about 1 inch (2.5 cm) from bottom, almost but not quite through to other side. If roast is not 1 inch (2.5 cm) thick, cover with plastic wrap and beat with a meat mallet to desired thickness. Season with cinnamon, sage, first amount of salt and pepper. Set aside.

Melt first amount of butter in a medium sized heavy bottomed pan over medium. Toss in shallots, garlic and apple, and cook for 1 minute. Add parsley, vinegar, salt and stock. Bring to a boil and gradually stir in cornmeal. Lower heat and stir until mixture is well combined and thick. Stir in cheese. Pour mixture into a small loaf pan. Cool in refrigerator until firm, about 30 minutes.

Meanwhile, gently wilt spinach in a small pot and set aside.

Transfer polenta to a cutting board and slice into two 1 x 1 inch (2.5 x 2.5 cm) rectangles approximately same length as pork loin. Lay one on edge of loin followed by a row of wilted spinach, and roll pork over polenta and spinach. Repeat step rolling pork loin into a complete cylinder. Tie with butcher twine. Sear in an oven-safe heavy bottomed pan over medium-high until all sides are golden brown. Place pan in 350°F (175°C) oven and bake for 70 minutes or until internal temperature reaches 165°F (74°C). Remove pork from pan and let rest on a wire rack. Add white wine to pan and reduce by half, then gradually whisk in remaining butter and mustard. Remove butcher twine from pork loin and cut into 1/2 inch (12 mm) slices. Drizzle with pan sauce. Makes 6 servings.

1 serving: *570 Calories; 30 g Total Fat (12 g Mono, 3 g Poly, 12 g Sat); 145 mg Cholesterol; 24 g Carbohydrate (2 g Fibre, 4 g Sugar); 44 g Protein; 440 mg Sodium*

Redneck Ribs

Tasty, tender ribs with southern smoked spices that will please the whole family.
Pineapple juice helps tenderize the pork, and peanuts give it a unique crunch.

Pork rib sections, 10 to 13 ribs each	2	2
Pork stock, water or mixture of both	6 cups	1.5 L
Pineapple juice	2 cups	500 mL
Bay leaves	2	2
Peppercorns	10	10
Garlic cloves, halved	5	5
Brown sugar	1/4 cup	60 mL
Salt	1 tsp.	5 mL
Tomato paste	1/2 cup	125 mL
Honey	1/4 cup	60 mL
Agave syrup	2 tbsp.	30 mL
Ground cinnamon	1/4 tsp.	1 mL
Ground cloves	1/8 tsp.	0.5 mL
Smoked paprika	1/2 tsp.	2 mL
Hot sauce	2 tsp.	10 mL
Prepared mustard	1 tbsp.	15 mL
Chopped unsalted peanuts	1/4 cup	60 mL

In a large roasting pan, lay ribs down flat. Mix together next 7 ingredients. Pour over ribs; the liquid should almost fully cover ribs—add more water to pan if necessary. Roast in 350°F (175°C) oven until meat begins to become loose on the bone, about 1 1/2 hours. Remove roasted pork from pan and set aside. Strain liquid though a fine-mesh sieve, and transfer 3 cups (750 mL) liquid to a large pan (reserve remaining liquid for other cooking purposes; see Tip). Place pan over high heat and reduce by three-quarters. Set aside to cool.

In a medium bowl, combine liquid reduction and next 8 ingredients. Fold in chopped nuts. Increase oven heat to 400°F (200°C). Brush sauce generously over ribs and return to oven. Bake for 10 minutes, then brush again with sauce and bake for an additional 10 minutes. Remove and let cool for 4 minutes. Makes 5 servings.

1 serving: 590 Calories; 15 g Total Fat (6 g Mono, 2 g Poly, 4 g Sat); 150 mg Cholesterol;
49 g Carbohydrate (2 g Fibre, 36 g Sugar); 64 g Protein; 1000 mg Sodium

Tip: The liquid reserved from roasting ribs can be used for a number of purposes including soup, sauces or even to spruce up your next pasta dish. It will keep in the fridge for up to 4 days or in the freezer for up to 6 months.

Soft Sweetie Pork Stew

No time to cook? No problem. Just toss all the ingredients for this dish in a slow cooker, let it take care of itself, and come home to a delicious, satisfying meal.

Butter	1 tbsp.	15 mL
Boneless pork shoulder, cut into 1 inch (2.5 cm) cubes	2 lbs.	900 g
Pineapple juice	1 cup	250 mL
Barbecue sauce	1/2 cup	125 mL
Tomato paste	1/4 cup	60 mL
Pork stock	4 cups	1 L
Low-sodium soy sauce	2 tbsp.	30 mL
Balsamic vinegar	2 tbsp.	30 mL
Agave syrup	2 tbsp.	30 mL
Salt	1/4 tsp.	1 mL
Pepper	1/4 tsp.	1 mL
Ground cloves	1/8 tsp.	0.5 mL
Ground cinnamon	1/8 tsp.	0.5 mL
Diced carrot	1 cup	250 mL
White mushrooms, quartered	2 cups	500 mL
Thinly sliced leek (white part only)	1 cup	250 mL
Fresh kernel corn	1/2 cup	125 mL
Chopped fresh sage	2 tbsp.	30 mL

Melt butter in a heavy bottomed pot over medium-high. Add pork and brown generously. Add pineapple juice and reduce by three-quarters.

Combine next 10 ingredients in a slow cooker. Add pork. Liquid should just cover pork—add more water if necessary. Cook on High until pork is tender and can be easily torn with a fork, about 2 1/2 hours.

Once pork is tender, add carrots, mushrooms and leeks. Stir well and cook for an additional 45 minutes.

Remove from heat and add corn and sage. Let rest for 10 minutes. Makes 6 servings.

1 serving: 490 Calories; 30 g Total Fat (13 g Mono, 3 g Poly, 11 g Sat); 95 mg Cholesterol; 27 g Carbohydrate (2 g Fibre, 8 g Sugar); 30 g Protein; 740 mg Sodium

Rack of Lamb with Blue Cheese Mushroom Ragout

A powerful, savoury dish combining creamy mushrooms with pan-roasted rack of lamb. This delicious meal is high in protein, zinc and B vitamins.

Racks of lamb, trimmed and frenched	2	2
Salt	1/2 tsp.	2 mL
Pepper	1/4 tsp.	1 mL
Finely diced fresh rosemary	1/2 tsp.	2 mL
Vegetable oil	1 tbsp.	15 mL
Butter	1 tbsp.	15 mL
Portobello mushrooms, gills removed, small dice	2	2
Shallots, finely diced	2	2
Sherry	1/4 cup	60 mL
Garlic cloves, minced	2	2
Grainy Dijon mustard	1 tsp.	5 mL
18% cream	1/2 cup	125 mL
Stilton cheese	2 oz.	57 g
Lemon juice	1 tsp.	5 mL
Whole natural almonds, grated	10	10

Cut lamb racks into 2-rib sections and season with salt, pepper and rosemary. Heat oil in an oven-safe heavy bottomed pan on medium and sear lamb sections, fat side down, until golden, about 2 minutes. Flip each lamb section and place pan in 450°F (230°C) oven for 9 to 10 minutes.

Melt butter in a large heavy bottomed pot over high heat. Add mushrooms and sauté for 4 minutes, allowing them to brown. Add shallots and pour in sherry. Mix well and allow moisture to evaporate until almost dry. Lower heat and add garlic and mustard. Cook for an additional minute. Add cream and cheese. Mix well and adjust heat to medium, reducing until mushrooms are coated with sauce, about 5 to 6 minutes. Stir in lemon juice.

Remove lamb from oven once desired doneness is reached and let rest for 5 minutes. Cut each 2-rib section in half and spoon mushroom ragout over top of each cut. Garnish with grated almonds. Makes 4 servings.

1 serving: 420 Calories; 29 g Total Fat (10 g Mono, 2 g Poly, 14 g Sat); 135 mg Cholesterol; 8 g Carbohydrate (1 g Fibre, 2 g Sugar); 33 g Protein; 580 mg Sodium

Tip: Racks of lamb can be found in your local grocery store, either fresh or frozen. Typically you will find them trimmed of excess fat and frenched—which is the process of removing flesh clean from the bone for visual appeal and ease of eating.

Chicken Coconut Curry

A modernized twist on a Indian classic, this recipe uses a creamy curry to blend the flavours of stewed chicken, onions, spinach, tomatoes and garlic. Tasty without being too spicy, this dish will appeal to adult and child alike, and busy cooks love the ease of preparation. Just sit back and let this meal take care of itself.

Boneless, skinless chicken breast, large dice	1 1/2 lbs.	680 g
Curry powder	1 tsp.	5 mL
Paprika	1 tsp.	5 mL
Ground cinnamon	1/4 tsp.	1 mL
Ground cumin	1/4 tsp.	1 mL
Ground cloves	1/8 tsp.	0.5 mL
Cayenne pepper	1/8 tsp.	0.5 mL
Salt	3/4 tsp.	4 mL
Pepper	1/2 tsp.	2 mL
White onion, diced	1	1
Carrots, julienned	3	3
Tomato, diced	1	1
Garlic cloves, minced	4	4
Coconut milk	1/2 cup	125 mL
Brown sugar	1 tbsp.	15 mL
Tomato paste	1/2 cup	125 mL
Brown rice	1 cup	250 mL
Boiling water	1 1/4 cups	300 mL
Fresh spinach leaves, lightly packed	3 cups	750 mL
Raw cashews	7 oz.	200 g
Chopped fresh cilantro	2 tbsp.	30 mL

Add first 16 ingredients to a large Dutch oven. Cook on medium-high for 3 to 5 hours.

Add brown rice and boiling water and cook for another 45 minutes or until rice is tender.

Fold in spinach and cook for another 2 minutes or until spinach has wilted. Garnish with cashews and cilantro. Makes 6 servings.

1 serving: 520 Calories; 21 g Total Fat (8 g Mono, 3 g Poly, 7 g Sat); 65 mg Cholesterol; 50 g Carbohydrate (7 g Fibre, 10 g Sugar); 37 g Protein; 470 mg Sodium

Spicy Jack Chicken

Crispy seasoned chicken baked with much less fat than popular fast-food varieties. This high protein meal is the perfect combination of sweet and spicy, with a splash of whisky to boot. It is ridiculously easy to prepare and pairs exceptionally well with polenta. If you don't have quinoa flour, use whole grain or whole wheat flour.

Eggs	2	2
Lemon juice	1 tsp.	5 mL
Quinoa flour	1/2 cup	125 mL
Dried oregano	1 tsp.	5 mL
Paprika	1/4 tsp.	1 mL
Salt	1/4 tsp.	1 mL
Pepper	1/4 tsp.	1 mL
Boneless, skinless chicken breasts	4	4
Jalapeño havarti cheese, cut into 4 skinny rectangles	3 oz.	85 g
Butter	1 tbsp.	15 mL
Butter	1 tsp.	5 mL
Canned kernel corn	1/2 cup	125 mL
Southern whisky (such as Jack Daniels)	3/4 cup	175 mL
Louisiana hot sauce	1/4 cup	60 mL
Water	1/4 cup	60 mL

Mix eggs and lemon juice on a large plate. In a medium bowl, combine flour, oregano, paprika, salt and pepper, and pour half of mixture onto a second large plate.

Cut a small horizontal slit in top of chicken breasts and stuff in 1 cheese slice per breast. Dredge chicken first in flour mixture, then egg mixture, then back in flour mixture, adding more flour mixture to the second plate as needed.

Add first amount of butter to a large heavy bottomed cast iron pan over medium-high. Sear chicken until browned on bottom, then flip each breast over and place pan in 400°F (200°C) oven. Bake for 10 minutes. Flip chicken over and continue to bake for another 8 to 10 minutes, until internal temperature of chicken is 165°F (74°C). Remove from pan, set on a cooling rack and cover with foil.

Return pan to heat and add remaining butter. It should instantly sizzle. Add corn and toss vigorously. Pour in whisky, hot sauce and water. Reduce by half. Sauce should be thick enough to coat the back of a spoon. To serve, cut each breast into thirds on a bias and drizzle with sauce. Makes 4 servings.

1 serving: 620 Calories; 19 g Total Fat (4.5 g Mono, 1.5 g Poly, 10 g Sat); 295 mg Cholesterol; 15 g Carbohydrate (3 g Fibre, 1 g Sugar); 69 g Protein; 580 mg Sodium

Tip: Having your pan and oven hot before adding your ingredients makes a significant difference in the quality

Chili Chicken Vermicelli

Sweet and spicy chicken paired with cool cucumber and pineapple. Delicious and economical—perfect university student fare!

Red jalapeños	2	2
Garlic cloves, chopped	3	3
Lemon juice	1 tsp.	5 mL
Lemon zest	1 tsp.	5 mL
Sugar	1/4 cup	60 mL
Agave syrup	2 tbsp.	30 mL
White wine vinegar	1/4 cup	60 mL
Water	3/4 cup	175 mL
Water	2 tbsp.	30 mL
Arrowroot	2 tsp.	10 mL
Vegetable oil	1 tbsp.	15 mL
Boneless, skinless chicken breast, large dice	2 lbs.	900 g
Dried vermicelli	8 oz.	250 g
Diced cucumber	1/2 cup	125 mL
Diced pineapple	1/2 cup	125 mL
Black and white sesame seeds	2 tbsp.	30 mL

For the chili sauce, place first 8 ingredients in a blender and blend until combined. Transfer to a large heavy bottomed pan and bring to a boil, then lower to a simmer.

Make a paste with remaining water and arrowroot. Mix paste into sauce and let thicken. Continue to simmer for another 5 minutes.

Heat oil in a medium pan over medium-high. Add chicken and sauté until cooked.

Set a large pot of water on stove to boil. Toss vermicelli into boiling water and cook for about 1 1/2 minutes, then remove from water.

Combine chicken, cucumber, pineapple and chili sauce in a large bowl. Pour over vermicelli on individual plates. Garnish with sesame seeds. Makes 6 servings.

1 serving: 400 Calories; 4.5 g Total Fat (1.5 g Mono, 1 g Poly, 1 g Sat); 105 mg Cholesterol; 49 g Carbohydrate (2 g Fibre, 12 g Sugar); 39 g Protein; 460 mg Sodium

Tip: To save some time making this dish, you can use a premade sweet chili sauce; there are many quality products on the market. If you do decide to make your own sauce, you can control its heat by adding more seeds from the jalapeño for more heat or less seeds for less heat.

Creamy Chicken Couscous

An attractive, high-protein meal with less fat than you might expect. A good source of calcium and vitamin C.

Water	1 1/2 cups	375 mL
Salt	1/4 tsp.	1 mL
Head of broccoli, cut into small florets	1	1
Israeli couscous	1 cup	250 mL
Butter	1 tbsp.	15 mL
Boneless, skinless chicken breast, diced	1	1
Garlic cloves, minced	2	2
Salt	1/4 tsp.	1 mL
Pepper	1/8 tsp.	0.5 mL
Fresh nutmeg	1/8 tsp.	0.5 mL
Arrowroot	2 tbsp.	30 mL
Milk	1 1/2 cups	375 mL
Light cream cheese	1/4 cup	60 mL
Lemon juice	2 tbsp.	30 mL
Fresh green beans, cut on a bias	10	10
Pine nuts	3 tbsp.	45 mL

In a large pot, bring water to a boil and add first amount of salt. Toss in broccoli, making sure it is submerged completely in water, cover with lid and cook for 2 minutes. Remove with a slotted spoon and let cool on a plate.

Return pot of water to stove and stir in couscous. Bring to a boil, then lower to a simmer. Cook until tender with a mild crunch, roughly 10 to 12 minutes.

Melt butter in a medium sized heavy bottomed pan on high. Add chicken and brown in pan. Lower heat to medium and mix in broccoli, garlic, remaining salt, pepper and nutmeg.

Place arrowroot in a small bowl and gradually whisk in milk until completely combined. Pour into saucepan. Mix in cream cheese and lemon juice. Fold in couscous. Plate individual portions and garnish with green beans and pine nuts. Makes 3 servings.

1 serving: 530 Calories; 18 g Total Fat (2.5 g Mono, 3 g Poly, 7 g Sat); 60 mg Cholesterol; 75 g Carbohydrate (4 g Fibre, 10 g Sugar); 28 g Protein; 620 mg Sodium

Lemon-baked Turkey

This may be the most universal recipe in the book. You can add this turkey to almost any dish. Try adding it to soups, salads, sandwiches and wraps for an extra boost of lean protein. It also freezes well.

Garlic cloves, halved	6	6
Brown sugar	1 tbsp.	15 mL
Chopped fresh thyme	1/2 tsp.	2 mL
Salt	1/2 tsp.	2 mL
Pepper	1/4 tsp.	1 mL
Olive oil	2 tbsp.	30 mL
Whole boneless, skinless turkey breast	1	1
Lemons	3	3

Combine first 6 ingredients in a large resealable bag. Add turkey. Cut lemons in half and squeeze juice into bag, then add rest of lemon. Seal bag and place in fridge for 1 to 6 hours—the longer the better. Remove turkey from bag and discard any pieces of garlic stuck to breast. Place turkey on a large baking sheet. Bake in 300°F (150°C) oven for 30 minutes, then broil on high heat for 5 minutes. The finished product will be lightly browned on outside and white throughout. Let rest for 5 minutes. Slice thin and serve. Makes 5 servings.

1 serving: 300 Calories; 16 g Total Fat (8 g Mono, 3 g Poly, 3.5 g Sat); 95 mg Cholesterol; 95 g Carbohydrate (1 g Fibre, 3 g Sugar); 32 g Protein; 320 mg Sodium

Turkey Tacos

These tasty tacos can be on the table in about 15 minutes. A great family meal, even more fun if the kids assemble their own.

Cooking oil	1 tsp.	5 mL
Lean ground turkey thigh	1/2 lb.	225 g
Frozen kernel corn, thawed	1/2 cup	125 mL
Salsa	1/2 cup	125 mL
Grated Mexican cheese blend	3/4 cup	175 mL
Hard taco shells	8	8
Shredded romaine lettuce, lightly packed	1 cup	250 mL
Diced tomato	1/2 cup	125 mL
Diced avocado (about 1/2 fruit)	1/2 cup	125 mL

Heat cooking oil in large frying pan on medium-high. Add turkey. Scramble-fry for about 8 minutes until browned.

Add corn and salsa. Reduce heat to medium. Cook for about 2 minutes, stirring occasionally, until liquid is evaporated. Stir in cheese.

Arrange taco shells on ungreased baking sheet. Bake in 400°F (200°C) oven for about 5 minutes until warm.

Place lettuce in taco shells. Top with turkey mixture, tomato and avocado. Makes 8 tacos.

1 taco: 170 Calories; 10 g Total Fat (1.5 g Mono, 0 g Poly, 3 g Sat); 25 mg Cholesterol; 13 g Carbohydrate (2 g Fibre, 2 g Sugar); 9 g Protein; 250 mg Sodium

Ginger Pineapple Meatballs

These tangy meatballs are not too sweet, not too sour and not too spicy. Serve over rice.

Large egg, fork beaten	1	1
Fine dry bread crumbs	1/2 cup	125 mL
Diced red pepper	1/4 cup	60 mL
Grated onion	1/4 cup	60 mL
Ground ginger	1/2 tsp.	2 mL
No-salt seasoning	1/2 tsp.	2 mL
Pepper	1/4 tsp.	1 mL
Lean ground turkey	1 lb.	454 g
Cooking oil	2 tsp.	10 mL
14 oz. (398 mL) can of crushed pineapple, with juice	1	1
Sweet chili sauce	1/2 cup	125 mL
Lime juice	1 tbsp.	15 mL
Grated ginger root	2 tsp.	10 mL
Salt	1/4 tsp.	1 mL
Low-sodium soy sauce	1 tbsp.	15 mL
Cornstarch	2 tsp.	10 mL
Sliced green onion	1/4 cup	60 mL

Combine first 7 ingredients in a medium bowl. Add turkey. Mix well. Roll into 1 inch (2.5 cm) balls. Heat cooking oil in large frying pan on medium-high. Add meatballs and cook for 5 to 10 minutes, turning often, until fully cooked and internal temperature reaches 175°F (80°C). Transfer with a slotted spoon to a plate lined with paper towel to drain.

Add next 5 ingredients to same frying pan. Stir soy sauce into cornstarch in a small cup. Add to pineapple mixture. Heat, stirring, until boiling and thickened. Reduce heat to medium-low, and stir in meatballs. Cook for about 5 minutes until heated through. Sprinkle with green onion before serving. Makes 4 servings.

1 serving: 350 Calories; 6 g Total Fat (2 g Mono, 1 g Poly, 1 g Sat); 115 mg Cholesterol; 44 g Carbohydrate (2 g Fibre, 28 g Sugar); 30 g Protein; 530 mg Sodium

Coconut Alfredo Pasta with Seared Scallops

A healthier take on the classic Alfredo sauce. Creamy and delicious, this dish is a good source of calcium, vitamin C and vitamin B12.

Whole grain pasta	8 oz.	250 g
Butter	1 tbsp.	15 mL
Large scallops	12	12
Thinly sliced leek (white part only)	1/4 cup	60 mL
Garlic cloves, minced	3	3
Broccoli florets	1/2 cup	125 mL
Shredded coconut	1/4 cup	60 mL
Arrowroot	1 tbsp.	15 mL
Milk	1 1/4 cups	300 mL
Coconut milk	3 tbsp.	45 mL
Lemon juice	1 tbsp.	15 mL
Salt	1/4 tsp.	1 mL
Pepper	1/4 tsp.	1 mL
Ground nutmeg	1/8 tsp.	0.5 mL
White Cheddar cheese, grated	4 oz.	113 g

Cook pasta according to package directions and set aside.

Melt butter in a heavy bottomed pan over medium-high. Add scallops and caramelize to a dark brown on top and bottom. Remove from pan and set aside. Add leeks to pan and lower heat to medium. Cook leeks until soft, about 2 minutes. Stir in garlic, broccoli and coconut and cook for an additional 2 minutes.

Add arrowroot to a small bowl and gradually whisk in milk. Pour mixture into pan and let thicken. Season with coconut milk, lemon juice, salt, pepper and nutmeg. Add cooked scallops and remove from heat. Let rest for 3 minutes.

To serve, divide pasta among 4 plates and spoon sauce mixture generously over top. Garnish with cheese. Makes 4 servings.

1 serving: 430 Calories; 19 g Total Fat (1 g Mono, 0 g Poly, 12 g Sat); 50 mg Cholesterol; 41 g Carbohydrate (9 g Fibre, 4 g Sugar); 24 g Protein; 290 mg Sodium

Crispy Cilantro Fish Cakes

A squeeze of lime brightens the curry and garlic flavour in these delicate cakes. We used haddock because of its availability, but mullet, mackerel or John Dory could be used instead.

Large egg	1	1
Chopped fresh cilantro	3 tbsp.	45 mL
Fish sauce	1 tbsp.	15 mL
Thai red curry paste	2 tsp.	10 mL
Garlic cloves, minced	3	3
Salt	1/4 tsp.	1 mL
Pepper	1/2 tsp.	2 mL
Haddock fillets, coarsely chopped	3/4 lb.	340 g
Panko bread crumbs	1 cup	250 mL
Cooking oil	1 cup	250 mL

Process first 7 ingredients in a blender or food processor until just combined. Add fish and process until coarsely ground.

Transfer fish mixture to medium bowl. Add 1/2 cup (125 mL) panko crumbs and mix well. Form into 1 inch (2.5 cm) balls and flatten into patties. Press patties into remaining 1/2 cup (125 mL) panko crumbs until coated.

Heat cooking oil in a large frying pan on medium-high. Shallow-fry patties in 2 batches for 1 to 2 minutes per side until browned. Transfer to paper towels to drain. Makes about 26 fish cakes.

1 cake: 30 calories; 1.5 g Total Fat (0.5 g Mono, 0.7 g Poly, 0.3 g Sat); 15 mg Cholesterol; 2 g Carbohydrate (trace Fibre, trace Sugar); 3 g Protein; 104 mg Sodium

Grilled Crandrizzle Salmon

A moist salmon fillet topped with a crunchy berry salsa. A tasty way to get a healthy dose of essential fatty acids and antioxidants. This colourful dish is especially eye-catching when garnished with a little fresh thyme.

Fresh salmon fillets, skin removed	2 lbs.	900 g
Prepared mustard	1 tbsp.	15 mL
Brown sugar	2 tbsp.	30 mL
Salt	1/4 tsp.	1 mL
Pepper	1/4 tsp.	1 mL
Diced fresh rosemary	1/4 tsp.	1 mL
Cranberry juice	1/4 cup	60 mL
Water	1/2 cup	125 mL
Raspberry vinegar	2 tbsp.	30 mL
Dried cranberries	1/2 cup	125 mL
Butter, softened	1/4 cup	60 mL
Butter	1 tbsp.	15 mL
Chopped almonds	1/2 cup	125 mL
Chopped fresh thyme	1 tsp.	5 mL
Poppy seeds	1 tsp.	5 mL
Maple syrup	2 tbsp.	30 mL

Cut salmon fillet into 5 equal pieces according to weight. In a small bowl combine next 6 ingredients. Smooth mixture over salmon and marinate for 30 minutes.

In a heavy bottomed pot, bring water and vinegar to a boil. Stir in cranberries and remove from heat. Cover with plastic wrap and steep for 20 minutes.

Preheat grill. Remove salmon fillets from marinade, and set remaining marinade aside. Brush a small section of hot grill with first amount of butter and gently place a fillet of salmon over top. Repeat with remaining fillets and adjust heat to medium-high. Cook for 2 minutes, then rotate salmon 90 degrees to acquire cross-pattern grill marks. Cook for another 2 minutes, then flip salmon over and cook until it is firm with a moist centre, about 3 to 5 minutes. Remove from heat and keep warm.

Melt remaining butter in a medium sized heavy bottomed saucepan over medium-high. Add almonds and cook until slightly brown. Add 2 tbsp. (30 mL) marinade. Lower heat and add rehydrated cranberries, thyme, poppy seeds and maple syrup. Generously spoon mixture over each fillet. Makes 5 servings.

1 serving: *470 Calories; 25 g Total Fat (9 g Mono, 6 g Poly, 7 g Sat); 120 mg Cholesterol;*
22 g Carbohydrate (2 g Fibre, 19 g Sugar); 39 g Protein; 290 mg Sodium

Tip: Grilling salmon is a delicate process. Be sure to brush the grill and the
fish with butter continually during the cooking process to prevent the
salmon from sticking to the grill.

Poached Trout with Salsa Rouge

In this relatively low-fat dish, softly poached trout is paired with a sweet pepper salsa. A great source of protein, vitamin C and vitamin B12. In the photo, it is shown served with mixed greens.

Balsamic vinegar	1/2 cup	125 mL
Honey	1 tbsp.	15 mL
Pine nuts	1/2 cup	125 mL
Roasted red peppers	1/4 cup	60 mL
Grainy Dijon mustard	1 tsp.	5 mL
Chopped fresh parsley	2 tbsp.	30 mL
Smoked (sweet) paprika	1/2 tsp.	2 mL
Cayenne pepper	1/8 tsp.	0.5 mL
Ground cloves	1/8 tsp.	0.5 mL
Melted butter	2 tbsp.	30 mL
White wine	2 cups	500 mL
Lemon juice	3 tbsp.	45 mL
Lemon zest	1 tbsp.	15 mL
Salt	1/4 tsp.	1 mL
Saffron threads (optional)	7	7
Vegetable stock or water	4 cups	1 L
Fresh trout fillets	6	6

Pour vinegar into a small saucepan and cook over medium until reduced by half and a syrupy consistency. Stir in honey and transfer to a small squeeze bottle.

For the salsa, place pine nuts in a food processor or blender and pulse until chunky. Add next 6 ingredients and blend. Gradually pour in melted butter. Transfer to a small bowl and set aside.

Combine next 6 ingredients in a medium pot and bring to a boil.

Lay trout flat in a roasting pan large enough to contain all fillets without overlapping. Pour boiling wine mixture over trout so fillets are fully submerged. If more liquid is needed, add hot tap water. Bake in 350°F (175°C) oven for 11 to 13 minutes, or until fish is just firm. Remove from oven and leave trout in liquid to rest for 5 minutes. To serve, spoon salsa over each fillet and drizzle with balsamic reduction. Makes 6 servings.

1 serving: 460 Calories; 23 g Total Fat (9 g Mono, 7 g Poly, 4.5 g Sat); 110 mg Cholesterol; 11 g Carbohydrate (1 g Fibre, 7 g Sugar); 38 g Protein; 260 mg Sodium

Seared Halibut with Shocked Onions and Chipotle Aioli

An interesting match of flavours and textures make this dish unique. A great source of protein, omega 3 fatty acids and niacin.

Mayonnaise	1/2 cup	125 mL
Garlic cloves, minced	2	2
Lemon juice	1 tbsp.	15 mL
Dijon mustard	1 tsp.	5 mL
Large green olives, minced	2	2
Chipotle chili powder	1/4 tsp.	1 mL
Paprika	1/8 tsp.	0.5 mL
Fresh, thick halibut fillet, skin removed	2 lbs.	900 g
Salt	1/2 tsp.	2 mL
Ground pepper	1/4 tsp.	1 mL
Finely chopped fresh oregano	1/2 tsp.	2 mL
Red wine vinegar	1/4 cup	60 mL
Agave syrup	2 tbsp.	30 mL
Water	1 cup	250 mL
Whole peppercorns	10	10
Whole cloves	3	3
Bay leaf	1	1
Salt	1/8 tsp.	0.5 mL
Red onion, halved horizontally and sliced 1/16 inch (1.5 mm) thick	1	1
Butter	1 tbsp.	15 mL

For the aioli, combine first 7 ingredients in a small bowl. Set aside.

Cut halibut into 5 equal pieces by weight. Pat dry with paper towel and season with first amount of salt, pepper and oregano. Set aside.

In a small saucepan, bring vinegar, agave, water, peppercorns, cloves, bay leaf and remaining salt to a boil. Lower heat and simmer for about 15 minutes. Remove pot from stove and strain vinegar mixture into a medium bowl. Discard peppercorns, cloves and bay leaf. Return liquid to pot and bring to a boil. Add onion and remove from heat. Steep for 5 minutes. Remove onions with a slotted spoon and drop into a bowl of ice water. Set aside. Discard cooking liquid.

Melt butter in an oven-safe heavy bottomed pan over medium-high. Sear halibut until golden brown. Gently flip each fillet, and place pan in 400°F (200°C) oven. Bake until firm with a moist centre, about 10 minutes. Remove from oven and keep warm. Remove onions from ice water and place on a plate with paper towel to dry. Serve each halibut fillet with a dob of aioli and garnish with a nest of shocked onions. Makes 5 servings.

1 serving: 420 Calories; 23 g Total Fat (12 g Mono, 6 g Poly, 3.5 g Sat); 70 mg Cholesterol; 11 g Carbohydrate (1 g Fibre, 1 g Sugar); 38 g Protein; 550 mg Sodium

Peanut Thai-fry

Sautéed vegetables and edamame coated with a peanut butter sauce over a bed of whole grain brown rice. A complete, balanced meal for vegans, this dish provides hefty protein, vitamin K and folate.

Brown rice	2 cups	500 mL
Low-sodium soy sauce	1/2 cup	125 mL
Pineapple juice	1/4 cup	60 mL
Peanut butter	3 tbsp.	45 mL
Sesame oil	1 tsp.	5 mL
Vegetable stock or water	1/4 cup	60 mL
Vegetable oil	1 tbsp.	15 mL
Fresh white mushrooms, diced	1 cup	250 mL
Bok choy, cut into 1 inch (2.5 cm) squares	1 cup	250 mL
Carrots, julienned	2	2
Cornstarch	2 tsp.	10 mL
Edamame beans	1/2 cup	125 mL
Daikon sprouts	1 cup	250 mL
Parsley leaves	16	16
Chopped walnuts	1/4 cup	60 mL

Cook rice according to package directions. Set aside.

In a small bowl, whisk together next 5 ingredients. Set aside.

Heat oil in a large heavy bottomed pan over medium-high. Add mushrooms and sauté until they begin to brown. Add bok choy and carrot and continue to cook until carrots begin to sweat, about 3 minutes. Lower heat and sprinkle cornstarch over top of vegetables. Add sauce mixture and mix well. Allow sauce to come to a boil, then lower heat to a simmer. Fold in edamame and sprouts and cook for an additional minute.

Pour sauced vegetables over individual rice portions and garnish with parsley leaves and walnuts. Makes 4 servings.

1 serving: 580 Calories; 20 g Total Fat (3 g Mono, 4.5 g Poly, 2 g Sat); 0 mg Cholesterol; 94 g Carbohydrate (10 g Fibre, 6 g Sugar); 15 g Protein; 1300 mg Sodium

Pasta with Quinoa Red Sauce

Quinoa replaces beef in this vegetarian pasta dish, providing a comparable protein content but without the saturated fat. This sauce also has more fibre and B vitamins than your typical meat sauce. You won't even miss the beef!

Whole grain pasta	8 oz.	250 g
Olive oil	1 tbsp.	15 mL
Garlic cloves, thinly sliced	4	4
Diced carrot	1/4 cup	60 mL
Diced celery	1/2 cup	125 mL
Diced red onion	1/4 cup	60 mL
Diced tomato	1/2 cup	125 mL
Tomato paste	1/2 cup	125 mL
Red wine vinegar	2 tbsp.	30 mL
Salt	1/4 tsp.	1 mL
Pepper	1/4 tsp.	1 mL
Vegetable stock or water	1 cup	250 mL
Red quinoa, rinsed	1/3 cup	75 mL
Chopped fresh basil	2 tbsp.	30 mL
Chopped fresh oregano	2 tbsp.	30 mL
Parmesan cheese, shaved	4 oz.	113 g

Cook pasta according to package directions. Set aside.

Heat oil in a large heavy bottomed pot over medium. Add garlic and cook until it becomes fragrant without browning, about 1 minute. Add carrots, celery and onion and cook until vegetables sweat and onion is translucent. Mix in tomato, tomato paste, vinegar, salt and pepper. Bring sauce to a boil, then lower heat and simmer for 10 minutes. Puree sauce with a hand blender until smooth.

Pour vegetable stock and quinoa into sauce. Cook, covered, for 15 minutes, stirring occasionally, until quinoa has bloomed. Fold in basil and oregano, and let rest for 4 minutes. To serve, spoon quinoa red sauce over pasta and garnish with Parmesan. Makes 4 servings.

1 serving: 430 Calories; 15 g Total Fat (4.5 g Mono, 0.5 g Poly, 6 g Sat); 20 mg Cholesterol; 55 g Carbohydrate (12 g Fibre, 9 g Sugar); 22 g Protein; 730 mg Sodium

Tip: Be sure to rinse the quinoa under cold water before cooking or it will have a bitter taste.

Mushroom Lasagna

Creamy ricotta and mushrooms stuffed into layers of lasagna. Complemented with a cool tomato salad.

Lasagna noodles	12	12
Olive oil	2 tbsp.	30 mL
Butter	1 tbsp.	15 mL
Sliced fresh white mushrooms	3 cups	750 mL
Diced portobello mushrooms, stems and gills removed	3 cups	750 mL
White wine	1/2 cup	125 mL
Shallots, chopped	4	4
Garlic cloves, chopped	4	4
Lemon juice	1 tbsp.	15 mL
Chopped fresh rosemary	1/2 tsp.	5 mL
Ground cloves	1/8 tsp.	0.5 mL
Salt	1/4 tsp.	1 mL
All-purpose flour	3 tbsp.	45 mL
Milk	2 cups	500 mL
Ricotta cheese	1 cup	250 mL
Tomato sauce	2 cups	500 mL
Mozzarella cheese, grated	3/4 lb.	340 g
Roma tomatoes, sliced	4	4
Green onions, thinly sliced	2	2

Cook lasagna noodles according to package directions. Drizzle with olive oil to prevent them from sticking and lay flat on a baking sheet lined with parchment paper. Cover with damp paper towel and set aside.

Melt butter in a large heavy bottomed pan over medium-high. When butter begins to foam, add both mushrooms and cook until browned well on all sides. Deglaze pan by pouring in wine and reduce by half. Lower heat to medium and add shallots, garlic, lemon juice, rosemary, cloves and salt. Cook until liquid has evaporated.

Place flour in a tall, narrow glass and gradually whisk in milk until well combined. Pour into pan and cook until it reaches a boil and thickens. Simmer for 5 minutes, then remove from heat and set aside.

Lightly grease a 9 x 13 inch (23 x 33 cm) baking dish and assemble lasagna in the following sequence:

4 lasagna noodles, 1/3 mushroom mixture, 1/2 ricotta, 1/2 tomato sauce,
4 lasagna noodles, 1/3 mushroom mixture, 1/2 ricotta, 1/2 tomato sauce,
4 lasagna noodles, 1/3 mushroom mixture, mozzarella.

Crinkle a large sheet of parchment paper under cold water and place over top of the dish. Bake in 375°F (190°C) for 15 minutes, then remove paper and broil for an additional 4 minutes or until cheese is golden brown. Let rest for 5 minutes. Garnish with sliced fresh tomato and green onion. Makes 8 servings.

1 serving: 450 Calories; 20 g Total Fat (6 g Mono, 1 g Poly, 10 g Sat); 50 mg Cholesterol; 44 g Carbohydrate (4 g Fibre, 10 g Sugar); 24 g Protein; 660 mg Sodium

Pepper Quinoa Pizza

This distinctive, delicious quinoa crust is packed with protein and is gluten free.
The cauliflower crust is another great gluten-free option.

Vegetable stock	1 3/4 cup	425 mL
Quinoa	1 1/4 cups	300 mL
Cornstarch	1/4 cup	60 mL
Basil pesto	2 tbsp.	30 mL
Canola oil	2 tbsp.	30 mL
Yellow cornmeal	2 tbsp.	30 mL
Tomato sauce	1/2 cup	125 mL
Thinly sliced fresh white mushrooms	1 cup	250 mL
Diced red pepper	1 cup	250 mL
Diced yellow pepper	1 cup	250 mL
Grated Asiago cheese	3/4 cup	175 mL

Bring stock to a boil in a medium saucepan. Stir in quinoa. Reduce heat to medium-low and simmer, covered, for about 20 minutes, without stirring, until quinoa is tender and liquid is absorbed. Spread on a large plate to cool. Transfer to a food processor.

Add next 3 ingredients. Process until combined and mixture resembles dough.

Sprinkle cornmeal over a well-greased 12 inch (30 cm) pizza pan. Press quinoa mixture into pan. Bake on bottom rack in 450°F (230°C) oven for about 15 minutes until set and edges are dry.

Spread tomato sauce over crust. Scatter remaining 4 ingredients, in order given, over tomato sauce. Bake for about 20 minutes until cheese is melted and golden. Cuts into 8 wedges.

1 wedge: 230 Calories; 12 g Total Fat (2 g Mono, 1 g Poly, 3.5 g Sat); 15 mg Cholesterol;
24 g Carbohydrate (2 g Fibre, 2 g Sugar); 7 g Protein; 410 mg Sodium

Cauliflower Crust: Break a head of cauliflower into florets. Toss them into a food processor or blender with 3 cloves of garlic and process into medium crumbs, about 2 to 3 minutes. Steam the mixture for about 5 minutes to soften. Pour into a clean tea towel; squeeze out as much moisture as possible. Transfer to a large mixing bowl and stir in 2 lightly beaten eggs, 1/2 cup (125 mL) grated mozzarella cheese, 1/4 cup (60 mL) grated parmesan cheese and some chopped fresh herbs (basil and oregano work well). Press the mixture into a greased 12 inch (30 cm) pizza pan. Bake in 425°F (220°C) oven until golden around the edges, about 25 minutes. The dough can be fragile after it's been baked, so handle with care.

Ratatouille

A new take on a beloved classic, this dish abounds with lycopene, vitamin C and antioxidants. It pairs well with anything and reheats very well for leftovers.

Extra virgin olive oil	1 tbsp.	15 mL
Red onion, diced	1	1
Red peppers, diced	2	2
Zucchini, diced	2	2
Large eggplants, diced	2	2
Garlic cloves, finely chopped	2	2
Red wine	1/4 cup	60 mL
Tomato paste	1/2 cup	125 mL
Chopped fresh thyme	1 tsp.	5 mL
Bay leaves	2	2
Roma tomato, diced	1	1
Salt	1/2 tsp.	2 mL
Pepper	1/4 tsp.	1 mL
Lemon juice	1 tbsp.	15 mL
Agave syrup	1 tsp.	5 mL

Heat oil in a heavy bottomed pot over medium-high. Add onion and red pepper, and cook for 1 minute. Add zucchini, eggplant and garlic, and cook until vegetables begin to sweat. Pour in wine and tomato paste and mix well. Fold in remaining ingredients and lower heat. Cover, allowing to braise for 10 minutes, stirring occasionally. Remove bay leaves. Remove from heat and let rest for 5 minutes, then serve. Makes 6 servings.

1 serving: 190 Calories; 4.5 g Total Fat (2.5 g Mono, 1 g Poly, 0.5 g Sat); 0 mg Cholesterol; 36 g Carbohydrate (14 g Fibre, 17 g Sugar); 6 g Protein; 400 mg Sodium

Bandit Bean Garbonzo Salad

Indian, Mediterranean, Asian, North American—this recipe steals ingredients from all over the globe and is a good source of dietary fibre, protein, vitamin C and manganese.

Chickpeas	3 cups	750 mL
Canned mandarin orange segments	1/2 cup	125 mL
Parsley leaves, stems trimmed	1/2 cup	125 mL
Red onion, diced	1/2	1/2
Grated orange zest	2 tsp.	10 mL
Unsalted sunflower seeds	2 tbsp.	30 mL
Chopped almonds	1/4 cup	60 mL
White balsamic vinegar	2 tbsp.	30 mL
Orange juice	1 tbsp.	15 mL
Honey	2 tsp.	10 mL
Garlic clove, chopped	1	1
Chopped ginger root	1 tsp.	5 mL
Poppy seeds	1 tsp.	5 mL
Ground cumin	1/8 tsp.	0.5 mL
Olive oil	1/3 cup	75 mL
Parmesan cheese, grated	3 oz.	85 g

Combine first 7 ingredients in a large bowl. Set aside.

Using a blender or hand blender, combine next 7 ingredients. Gradually pour in olive oil until mixture is well combined.

To serve, pour dressing over chickpea mixture, using as much dressing as you desire, and garnish with Parmesan. Served chilled. Makes 6 servings.

1 serving: 410 Calories; 22 g Total Fat (12 g Mono, 3 g Poly, 4.5 g Sat); 10 mg Cholesterol; 39 g Carbohydrate (10 g Fibre, 8 g Sugar); 17 g Protein; 510 mg Sodium

Blue Ice Salad

A cool, crisp salad with blue cheese and sweet grapes. This stunning dish is dressy enough to wow guests at a dinner party. Pureed tofu gives the dressing a delicious creaminess without adding a lot of fat.

Bacon slices	3	3
Blue cheese (Stilton or Roquefort)	1/4 cup	60 mL
Light mayonnaise	1/4 cup	60 mL
Silken tofu	3 1/2 oz.	100 g
Poppy seeds	1 tsp.	5 mL
Chopped fresh basil	1 tbsp.	15 mL
Head of iceberg lettuce	1	1
Chopped walnuts	2 tbsp.	30 mL
Blue cheese (Stilton or Roquefort)	4 oz.	113 g
Red grapes, halved	1 cup	250 mL

Cook bacon and cut into a small dice. Set aside on paper towel.

Combine first amount of blue cheese, mayonnaise, tofu and poppy seeds in a blender and pulse until smooth. Fold in chopped basil. Set aside.

Cut lettuce into 4 equal sized wedges and gently loosen layers. Plate each individual salad by placing a dob of dressing on a plate followed by a wedge of lettuce. Spoon dressing generously over lettuce and garnish with diced bacon, walnuts, remaining 4 oz. (113 g) blue cheese and grapes. Served chilled. Makes 4 servings.

1 serving: 390 Calories; 32 g Total Fat (10 g Mono, 6 g Poly, 12 g Sat); 50 mg Cholesterol; 13 g Carbohydrate (2 g Fibre, 9 g Sugar); 15 g Protein; 870 mg Sodium

Cherry Slaw

Can't get your kids to eat their cabbage? Let this creamy cherry recipe change the way non–cabbage enthusiasts feel about this super nutritious vegetable. The slaw tastes even better the day after it is made.

Head of red cabbage	1/2	1/2
Julienned carrot	1 cup	250 mL
Chopped walnuts	1/4 cup	60 mL
Dried cherries	1/3 cup	75 mL
Light mayonnaise	1/4 cup	60 mL
Lemon juice	2 tbsp.	30 mL
Garlic cloves, minced	2	2
Red wine vinegar	1 tbsp.	15 mL

Cut cabbage into quarters and remove and discard core. Slice into 1/8 inch (3 mm) cuts. Toss with carrot, walnuts and dried cherries. Set aside.

Combine remaining 4 ingredients in a large bowl. Add cabbage mixture and mix well. Let sit at room temperature for 15 minutes to soften cabbage and combine flavours. Serve chilled. Makes 6 servings.

1 serving: 120 Calories; 7 g Total Fat (1.5 g Mono, 4 g Poly, 1 g Sat); trace Cholesterol; 14 g Carbohydrate (3 g Fibre, 8 g Sugar); 3 g Protein; 95 mg Sodium

Kale Caesar with Pumpkin Parmesan Crisps

A healthier alternative to your traditional Caesar salad. The addition of kale provides a boost of iron, manganese, fibre and vitamin K.

Heads of romaine lettuce	2	2
Bunch of kale	1	1
Grated Parmesan cheese	1/2 cup	125 mL
Chopped pumpkin seeds	1/4 cup	60 mL
Whole grain bread crust, cut into 1/2 inch (12 mm) cubes	1 cup	250 mL
Lemon juice	3 tbsp.	45 mL
Olive oil	2 tbsp.	30 mL
Chopped fresh thyme	1/2 tsp.	2 mL
Salt	1/4 tsp.	1 mL
Egg	1	1
Grainy Dijon mustard	1 tsp.	5 mL
Lemon juice	1 tbsp.	15 mL
Worcestershire sauce	1/2 tsp.	2 mL
Anchovy fillets	8	8
Garlic cloves, chopped	4	4
Cayenne pepper	1/8 tsp.	0.5 mL
Ground nutmeg	1/8 tsp.	0.5 mL
Flaxseed	1 tsp.	5 mL
Extra virgin olive oil	1/2 cup	125 mL
Lemon juice	1 tbsp.	15 mL

Cut romaine into 1 1/2 inch (3.8 cm) squares. Remove thick stems from kale and cut leaves into 1 inch (2.5 cm) squares. Rinse and spin dry.

Cover a baking tray with a sheet of parchment paper. Using a cookie cutter with a 2 inch (5 cm) diameter, shape cheese into circles and sprinkle each with pumpkin seeds. Gently place in 350°F (175°C) oven and bake for 8 to 10 minutes or until melted and golden. Set aside to cool.

In a medium bowl mix together bread crusts, first amount of lemon juice, olive oil, thyme and salt. Spread out evenly on a large baking sheet and bake for 10 to 12 minutes or until lightly browned and crisp.

For dressing, combine egg, mustard, second amount of lemon juice, Worcestershire sauce, anchovies, garlic, cayenne, nutmeg and flax seed. Blend until combined. Set blender to low speed and slowly add oil, then add remaining lemon juice. To serve, mix lettuce and kale with dressing to taste and top with parmesan crisps and croutons. Makes 6 servings.

1 serving: 380 Calories; 30 g Total Fat (19 g Mono, 4.5 g Poly, 6 g Sat); 45 mg Cholesterol; 21 g Carbohydrate (7 g Fibre, 5 g Sugar); 12 g Protein; 550 mg Sodium

Harvest Salad

A crisp, refreshing salad with sweetness of corn and beets. This filling salad can served as a side or can be a complete meal in itself.

Fresh beets	3	3
Fresh kernel corn	1/4 cup	60 mL
Bacon bits	1/4 cup	60 mL
Chopped walnuts	1/4 cup	60 mL
Flaxseed	1 tbsp.	15 mL
Chili powder	1/4 tsp.	1 mL
White balsamic vinegar	1/4 cup	60 mL
Dijon mustard	1 tbsp.	15 mL
Lemon juice	1 tbsp.	15 mL
Maple syrup	1 tbsp.	15 mL
Garlic cloves, minced	2	2
Egg	1	1
Fresh parsley leaves, stems removed	1/4 cup	60 mL
Salt	1/8 tsp.	0.5 mL
Olive oil	1/2 cup	125 mL
Heads of romaine lettuce, cut into 1 inch (2.5 cm) squares	3	3
Head of radicchio, cut into 1 inch (2.5 cm) squares	1	1
Green olives, diced	4	4
White Cheddar cheese, grated	4 oz.	113 g

Place beets in a shallow roasting pan and cover completely with foil. Roast in 400°F (200°C) oven until cooked but still firm, about 90 minutes. Transfer to a resealable bag and set aside to cool (see Tip). Remove tops from cooled beets and wipe with paper towel to remove skin, then cut into 1 x 1/8 inch (38 x 3 mm) crescents.

Combine next 5 ingredients. Place on a baking sheet lined with parchment paper and roast at 325°F (160°C) for 10 minutes. Set aside to cool.

For the dressing, combine next 8 ingredients in a tall narrow bowl and blend until smooth using a hand blender. Slowly pour in olive oil while blending to make an emulsion.

Combine dressing, lettuce, radicchio, corn mixture, beets and olives in a large bowl. Garnish with cheese. Serve chilled. Makes 6 servings.

1 serving: 400 Calories; 31 g Total Fat (14 g Mono, 5 g Poly, 8 g Sat); 60 mg Cholesterol; 22 g Carbohydrate (8 g Fibre, 10 g Sugar); 13 g Protein; 430 mg Sodium

Tip: When selecting beets for this recipe, look for ones similar in size. Placing the roasted beets in a resealable bag traps the steam, which helps loosen the skin, making the beets easier to peel.

Red Dragon Potato Salad

The nutrient- and fibre-rich potato has its time to shine in this vividly coloured recipe with accents of sweet red pepper and chipotle. With its mild spicing, even kids will love this dish.

Red potatoes, quartered	8	8
Roasted red peppers	1/4 cup	60 mL
Pine nuts	2 tbsp.	30 mL
Chopped fresh parsley	2 tbsp.	30 mL
Chipotle chili powder	1/4 tsp.	1 mL
Lemon juice	1 tbsp.	15 mL
Grainy Dijon mustard	1 tbsp.	15 mL
Light mayonnaise	3 tbsp.	45 mL
Stalk of celery, diced	1	1
Red pepper, diced	1	1
Green onions, thinly sliced	2	2

Place potatoes in a large pot and add cold water until potatoes are submerged. Bring to a boil over high heat, then lower to a simmer. Cook for 20 minutes or until potatoes are tender. Drain and allow potatoes to air dry on a baking sheet.

Add roasted red peppers, pine nuts, parsley, chipotle, lemon juice and mustard to a blender or food processor and blend until smooth. Fold in mayonnaise. Set aside.

Cut potatoes into 1/2 inch (12 mm) slices. Toss with celery, red pepper and onion. Spoon dressing over mixture and gently mix until coated. Serve cool. Makes 6 servings.

1 serving: 280 Calories; 4.5 g Total Fat (1 g Mono, 2.5 g Poly, 0.5 g Sat); trace Cholesterol; 54 g Carbohydrate (6 g Fibre, 4 g Sugar); 7 g Protein; 135 mg Sodium

Tip: Roasted red peppers can be found at your local grocery store, in canned or jarred forms. You can also make your own by roasting red bell peppers under a broiler or on a grill until charred. Cool peppers in a sealed resealable bag for 10 minutes, then scrape away skin and remove core and stem with a small knife.

Watermelon and Feta Salad

The expression "the whole is greater than the sum of its parts" could have been coined for this fantastic recipe. This fun, cool salad is so much more flavourful than you'd expect from the simplicity of the ingredients and the ease of preparation.

Balsamic vinegar	1 cup	250 mL
Basil leaves	1 cup	250 mL
Olive oil	3 tbsp.	45 mL
Large seedless watermelon	1/2	1/2
Feta cheese	10 oz.	285 g
Frisée, trimmed and cut into large pieces	1 cup	250 mL

Pour balsamic vinegar into a small heavy bottomed pot and set on high heat until reduced by half. Set aside to cool, then transfer to a small resealable bag or fine-tipped piping bag.

Add basil to a small grinder or blender. Blend while gradually adding oil until combined.

Cut watermelon vertically into 3/4 inch (2 cm) slices. Remove peel and cut flesh roughly into 2 inch (5 cm) triangles. Set aside. Cut feta into 1/2 inch (12 mm) slices and cut roughly into 1 inch (2.5 cm) triangles. Lay watermelon and feta on a large rectangular plate in a repeating sequence, i.e. watermelon, then feta, then watermelon and so on.

Poke a tiny hole in bottom corner of resealable bag containing vinegar reduction. Drizzle over top of watermelon and feta, then spoon drops of basil oil over top. Garnish with frisée. Serve chilled. Makes 6 servings.

1 serving: 330 Calories; 18 g Total Fat (7 g Mono, 1 g Poly, 8 g Sat); 45 mg Cholesterol; 36 g Carbohydrate (2 g Fibre; 31 g Sugar); 10 g Protein; 530 mg Sodium

Quinoa Mashed Potatoes

Mashed potatoes never looked so good! Quinoa adds a nutritious kick to the beloved classic. These potatoes are so healthy that you can add a little extra butter on the top before serving without feeling guilty.

Large russet potatoes, quartered	6	6
Chicken stock	1/2 cup	125 mL
Water	1/2 cup	125 mL
Bay leaf	1	1
Red quinoa, rinsed	1/2 cup	125 mL
Milk	3/4 cup	175 mL
Butter	2 tbsp.	30 mL
Salt	1/2 tsp.	2 mL
Pepper	1/4 tsp.	1 mL
Ground nutmeg	1/8 tsp.	0.5 mL
Lemon juice	2 tsp.	10 mL

Place quartered potatoes in a large heavy bottomed pot and add cold water until potatoes are submerged. Bring to a boil, then reduce to a simmer and cook for 25 minutes, or until potatoes are tender. Drain cooked potatoes and place on a baking sheet lined with parchment paper. Bake in 350°F (175°C) oven for 5 minutes to dry.

In a medium pot bring chicken stock, water and bay leaf to a boil. Stir in quinoa and simmer until cooked, about 12 minutes. Remove from heat and set aside.

Combine milk, butter, salt, pepper and nutmeg. Bring to a boil. Add potatoes and mash, then whisk aggressively until potatoes are light and fluffy. Fold in cooked quinoa and lemon juice. Makes 6 servings.

1 serving: 320 Calories; 5 g Total Fat (1 g Mono, 0 g Poly, 2.5 g Sat); 10 mg Cholesterol; 62 g Carbohydrate (6 g Fibre, 4 g Sugar); 9 g Protein; 260 mg Sodium

Rippin' Roasted Potatoes

Crispy oven roasted potatoes without all the extra fat that comes with deep frying. After trying this little beauties, you may just retire your fryer. This side dish pairs very well with fish and is an excellent source of vitamin A.

Red potatoes, quartered and sliced 1/4 inch (6 mm) thick	8	8
Canola oil	4 tsp.	20 mL
Chopped fresh thyme	1/4 tsp.	1 mL
Salt	1/2 tsp.	2 mL
Pepper	1/4 tsp.	1 mL
Paprika	1/4 tsp.	1 mL
Red wine vinegar	1 tbsp.	15 mL
Cornstarch	2 tbsp.	30 mL
Canola oil	2 tsp.	20 mL

Place a large baking tray in 450°F (230°C) oven. Toss potatoes with first amount of oil, thyme, salt, pepper, paprika and vinegar. Sprinkle 1 tbsp. (15 mL) cornstarch over potatoes and mix in, then repeat with remaining 1 tbsp. (15 mL) cornstarch.

Carefully remove hot baking tray from oven and pour remaining oil over top, then quickly spread potatoes out evenly. Bake for 15 minutes, then remove from oven and shuffle potatoes around. Return to oven and adjust heat to 500°F (260°C). Bake for an additional 15 minutes until golden brown and crispy. Let rest for 5 minutes before serving. Makes 6 servings.

1 serving: 270 Calories; 4.5 g Total Fat (3 g Mono, 1.5 g Poly, 0 g Sat); 0 mg Cholesterol; 52 g Carbohydrate (6 g Fibre, 2 g Sugar); 9 g Protein; 260 mg Sodium

Tip: To prevent sticking, it is important to have your baking tray piping hot before placing the potatoes on it. Also when shuffling the potatoes, use a thin metal spatula. Allowing the potatoes to rest after they have cooked helps lift them from the tray.

Warm Potato Salad with Morels and Melted Spinach

A warm, creamy salad rich in the B-complex vitamins as well as vitamins A and C. Pairs well with pork and chicken. If you can't find fresh morels, substitute button or cremini mushrooms.

Medium red potatoes	5	5
Butter	1 tbsp.	15 mL
Fresh morel mushrooms, rinsed and halved	1 cup	250 mL
Garlic clove, minced	1	1
Milk	1/2 cup	125 mL
Grainy Dijon mustard	1 tsp.	5 mL
Salt	1/2 tsp.	2 mL
Pepper	1/4 tsp.	1 mL
Arrowroot	2 tsp.	10 mL
Lemon juice	1 tbsp.	15 mL
Chopped fresh thyme	1 tsp.	5 mL
Chopped spinach	2 cups	500 mL
Pine nuts	1/4 cup	60 mL
Havarti cheese, grated	2 oz.	57 g

Cut potatoes into 1/2 inch (12 mm) cubes and toss into a medium pot. Add cool water until potatoes are just submerged. Place on high heat and bring to a boil. Lower heat to simmer and cook for 13 minutes, or until potatoes begin to soften. Remove and let dry on a large plate.

Melt butter in a large heavy bottomed pan over high heat. Add potatoes and cook until browned. Lower heat to medium and mix in mushrooms and garlic. Continue to cook until mushrooms soften, about 2 minutes.

Mix milk, mustard, salt and pepper in a small bowl and microwave until warm. Place arrowroot in a small bowl and gradually whisk in milk mixture. Once combined, add to pan with mushrooms and potatoes. Stir gently and lower heat.

Fold in lemon juice, thyme and spinach, and let wilt. Garnish with pine nuts and havarti. Serve warm. Makes 4 servings.

1 serving: 360 Calories; 15 g Total Fat (3.5 g Mono, 3 g Poly, 6 g Sat); 30 mg Cholesterol; 47 g Carbohydrate (6 g Fibre, 4 g Sugar); 12 g Protein; 830 mg Sodium

Wild Mushroom Risotto Cakes

A creamy mushroom and rice cake with a cheesy surprise. This dish is time consuming to prepare, but it is definitely worth the effort.

Chicken or vegetable stock or water	6 cups	1.5 L
Butter	2 tbsp.	30 mL
Chanterelle or oyster mushrooms, rough chop	1 cup	250 mL
Shallots, diced	2	2
Garlic cloves, diced	2	2
Chopped fresh rosemary	1/2 tsp.	2 mL
Arborio rice	1 1/2 cups	375 mL
White wine vinegar	1 tbsp.	15 mL
Lemon juice	2 tsp.	10 mL
Chopped fresh thyme	1/2 tsp.	2 mL
Salt	1/2 tsp.	2 mL
Grated Swiss cheese	1/2 cup	125 mL
Chopped fresh parsley	2 tbsp.	30 mL
Grainy Dijon mustard	1 tsp.	5 mL
Cubes of Cheddar cheese (3/4 inch, 2 cm)	8	8
Butter	1 tbsp.	15 mL

Bring stock to a boil in a large pot.

Melt first amount of butter in a large heavy bottomed pot over medium heat, then add mushrooms and cook until they begin to brown lightly. Mix in shallots, garlic and rosemary sauté lightly until shallots begin to sweat, about 2 minutes. Stir in rice and cook for an additional minute.

Add 1 ladle of stock to the rice mixture and stir vigorously. Once stock is absorbed, add another ladle. Repeat this process until all stock has been used and rice is tender, adding more hot tap water if necessary. Fold in vinegar, lemon juice, thyme, salt, Swiss cheese, parsley and mustard. Pour risotto onto a large tray or sheet and place in refrigerator until completely cool.

Preheat oven to high broil. Use a cookie cutter to shape cooled risotto into eight 3 inch (7.5 cm) cakes and punch a cube of Cheddar into centre of each one. Line a large baking sheet with parchment paper and grease lightly with remaining butter. Place cakes on tray and broil on middle rack in oven until cakes turn a golden brown, about 15 minutes. Flip cakes and repeat to brown bottom. Let cool for 5 minutes before serving. Makes 8 cakes.

1 cake: 190 Calories; 6 g Total Fat (1.5 g Mono, 0 g Poly, 4 g Sat); 20 mg Cholesterol; 29 g Carbohydrate (trace Fibre, 0 g Sugar); 5 g Protein; 200 mg Sodium

Tip: When cooking risotto, keep a close eye on your rice and remember to keep stirring throughout the whole process, scraping down the sides and bottom of the pan. If neglected, your risotto will not have the creamy texture it should, and it may burn to the bottom of the pan.

Wild Rice and Lentil Pilaf

A light summer dish with Indian spices and sweet mango. Rich in folate, thiamin, protein and dietary fibre.

Butter	2 tbsp.	30 mL
Diced mushrooms	1 cup	250 mL
White wine	1 cup	250 mL
Garlic cloves, minced	3	3
Chopped dried mango	2 tbsp.	30 mL
Coriander	1/4 tsp.	1 mL
Cumin	1/8 tsp.	0.5 mL
Green lentils	3/4 cup	175 mL
Wild rice or whole grain rice	1 1/2 cups	325 mL
Vegetable stock	6 cups	1.5 L
White onion, quartered	1/2	1/2
Bay leaves	2	2
Chopped almonds	2 tbsp.	30 mL
Chopped fresh cilantro	1 tbsp.	15 mL

Melt butter in a large heavy bottomed pan over medium-high. Sauté mushrooms until brown. Pour in white wine and reduce by three-quarters. Lower heat and add garlic, mango, coriander, cumin, lentils and rice. Cook for an additional 3 minutes on low heat to allow flavours to infuse.

Transfer to a medium sized casserole dish and pour stock over rice mixture. Stir in onion and bay leaves, cover and bake in 350°F (175°C) oven for 60 to 75 minutes or until lentils and rice become tender. Remove from oven and discard onion and bay leaves. Fluff with a fork, and garnish with almonds and cilantro. Makes 6 servings.

1 serving: 330 Calories; 6 g Total Fat (1 g Mono, 0 g Poly, 2.5 g Sat); 10 mg Cholesterol; 57 g Carbohydrate (7 g Fibre, 3 g Sugar); 9 g Protein; 35 mg Sodium

Grilled Zucchini with Chili and Mint

Not sure what to do with all that zucchini in your garden? Try this tantalizing combination of tender zucchini, hot peppers and cool mint. Not only will your senses be stirred, but you'll also get a healthy dose of B-complex vitamins.

Olive oil	3 tbsp.	45 mL
Lemon juice	1 tbsp.	15 mL
Chopped fresh mint	2 tbsp.	30 mL
Salt	1/4 tsp.	1 mL
Pepper	1/4 tsp.	1 mL
Chili flakes	1/4 tsp.	1 mL
Zucchini, sliced 1/4 inch (6 mm) thick on a bias	4	4
Salt	1/4 tsp.	1 mL

Preheat a grill on high. Whisk together oil, lemon juice, mint, first amount of salt, pepper and chili flakes. Brush mixture onto zucchini slices and lay out on grill. Char each slice lightly on both sides for about 1 1/2 minutes per side—zucchini should just begin to soften. Remove from grill and sprinkle with remaining salt. Makes 6 servings.

1 serving: 80 Calories; 7 g Total Fat (4.5 g Mono, 1 g Poly, 1 g Sat); 0 mg Cholesterol; 5 g Carbohydrate (2 g Fibre, 2 g Sugar); 2 g Protein; 170 mg Sodium

Tip: Zucchini cooks quickly and will continue to cook even once it is removed from the grill. Make sure your grill is very hot before adding the zucchini to get proper charring and to prevent it from getting mushy.

Melted Greens

Gently wilted greens with the essence of garlic make this an easy, nutrient-dense choice.

Lemon juice	1 tbsp.	15 mL
Swiss chard, thick veins removed	1/2 lb.	225 g
Spinach	1 lb.	454 g
Arugula	1/2 lb.	225 g
Garlic cloves, cracked with side of knife	4	4
Salt	1/8 tsp.	0.5 mL

Put all ingredients in a large pot over medium heat and cover with a lid. Steam, stirring frequently with tongs so that greens wilt evenly. Remove from heat once all greens are just wilted, and let rest for 4 minutes. Remove and discard garlic cloves. Makes 6 servings.

1 serving: 40 Calories; 0.5 g Total Fat (0 g Mono, 0 g Poly, 0 g Sat); 0 mg Cholesterol; 6 g Carbohydrate (3 g Fibre, 2 g Sugar); 4 g Protein; 200 mg Sodium

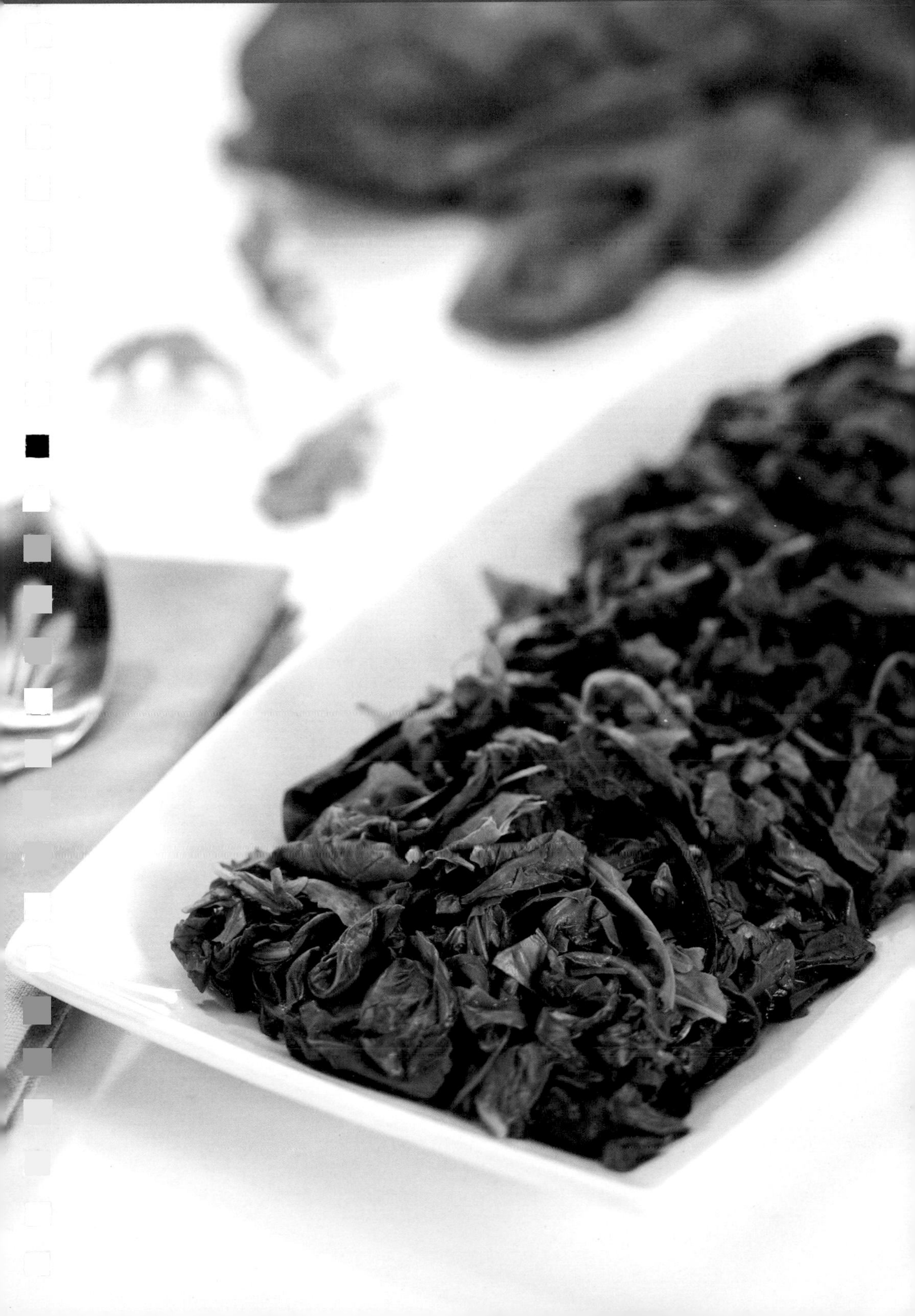

Cheesecake-stuffed Strawberries

Sweet, creamy strawberries stuffed with a simple cheesecake. As tasty as they are pretty, these treats are easy to prepare and loved by all.

Whole fresh strawberries	20	20
Light cream cheese, **at room temperature**	3/4 cup	175 mL
Vanilla extract	1 tsp.	5 mL
Balsamic vinegar	1 tbsp.	15 mL
Chopped walnuts	2 tbsp.	30 mL
Dark chocolate chips, melted	1/2 cup	125 mL

Cut off stems and core strawberries with a paring knife or tomato shark. Set aside.

In a medium bowl, whip cream cheese until fluffy. Fold in vanilla and balsamic vinegar. Using a piping bag, fill strawberries with cream cheese mixture. Roll the end of each strawberry in chopped walnuts, and drizzle with melted chocolate. Serve chilled. Makes 20 strawberries.

1 strawberry: 50 Calories; 3.5 g Total Fat (0 g Mono, 0 g Poly, 2 g Sat); 5 mg Cholesterol; 4 g Carbohydrate (trace Fibre, 3 g Sugar); 1 g Protein; 45 mg Sodium

Tip: For the fluffiest results, allow your cream cheese to warm to room temperature before whipping it.

Super Cookies

A nutritious cookie that is a definite hit with the kids. This cookie uses lower glycemic carbohydrates and has more fibre than your average chocolate chip cookie. Try making an extra-large batch by doubling or even tripling the recipe—these cookies freeze well and thaw in a few minutes.

Rolled oats	1 1/4 cup	300 mL
Flaxseed	2 tbsp.	30 mL
All-purpose flour	3/4 cup	175 mL
Whole wheat flour	1 cup	250 mL
Sugar	1/3 cup	75 mL
Baking powder	1 1/2 tsp.	7 mL
Ground cinnamon	1 tsp.	5 mL
Salt	1/4 tsp.	1 mL
Dark chocolate chips	1/2 cup	125 mL
Finely chopped, unpeeled red apple	1 cup	250 mL
Milk	3/4 cup	175 mL
Agave syrup	1/3 cup	75 mL
Melted butter	1/2 cup	125 mL
Egg	1	1

Add oats and flaxseed to a large bowl and sift in both flours, sugar, baking powder, cinnamon and salt. Fold in chocolate and apples. Make a well in the centre.

Whisk together milk, agave, melted butter and egg in a medium bowl. Add to well in dry mixture. Mix until just combined. Do not over mix. Drop by spoonful onto an ungreased baking sheet. Bake in 375°F (190°C) oven for 18 to 20 minutes or until cookies begin to brown lightly around the edges. Transfer to wire racks to cool. Makes 24 cookies.

1 cookie: 140 Calories; 6 g Total Fat (1.5 g Mono, 0.5 g Poly, 3.5 g Sat); 20 mg Cholesterol; 19 g Carbohydrate (2 g Fibre, 5 g Sugar); 2 g Protein; 70 mg Sodium

Tip: Use a gentle hand when mixing the wet and dry ingredients and stir until just combined. Excess mixing of the batter will result in dense, tough cookies.

Aloe Vera Soy Sorbet

Finally a creamy sorbet that a vegan can enjoy! Soy is paired with vanilla bean and cool aloe for a refreshing summer treat that contains many essential vitamins and minerals. No need to feel guilty about this pleasure!

Vanilla bean	**1**	**1**
Soy milk	**4 cups**	**1 L**
Aloe vera beverage	**2 cups**	**500 mL**
Sugar	**1/4 cup**	**60 mL**
Citrus-scented dark chocolate, roughly chopped	**1/2 cup**	**125 mL**

Slice vanilla bean vertically and scrape seeds away from bean with a paring knife, then add seeds and pod to a medium pot with soy milk, aloe beverage and sugar. Place pot over medium heat, and whisk continuously until sugar is dissolved and milk begins to scald. Transfer liquid to a container, then cool in an ice bath or place in refrigerator until cool.

Pour mixture into an ice cream machine and churn until the mixture becomes stiff. Fold in chocolate. Serve immediately or transfer to a cool bowl and freeze for later use. Makes 6 servings.

1 serving: 200 Calories; 8 g Total Fat (0.5 g Mono, 1.5 g Poly, 3 g Sat); 0 mg Cholesterol; 26 g Carbohydrate (2 g Fibre, 17 g Sugar); 8 g Protein; 95 mg Sodium

Tip: If you freeze this sorbet for later, move it from the freezer to the fridge an hour before serving so that it can soften.

Blueberry Apple Crisp

This warm, simple dessert goes well with a scoop of vanilla ice cream.

Fresh blueberries	1 cup	250 mL
Gala apples, cored and cut into 1/4 inch (6 mm) slices	10	10
Lemon juice	1/4 cup	60 mL
Agave syrup	1 tbsp.	15 mL
Arrowroot	1 tbsp.	15 mL
Ground cinnamon	1/2 tsp.	2 mL
Whole unsalted almonds	1 cup	250 mL
Rolled oats	1/2 cup	125 mL
Whole grain flour	1 cup	250 mL
Brown sugar	3/4 cup	175 mL
Salt	1/8 tsp.	0.5 mL
Baking soda	1/4 tsp.	1 mL
Butter	1/2 cup	125 mL

Combine first 6 ingredients in a large bowl. Transfer to a 10 x 15 inch (25 x 38 cm) baking dish. Set aside.

Add almonds to a food processor or blender and grind in pulses into a coarse texture. Transfer to a large bowl and add oats, flour, brown sugar, salt and baking soda. Melt butter and pour over mixture, then mix with your hands. Sprinkle evenly over apple mixture in baking dish. Bake in 375°F (190°C) oven for 45 minutes or until top is crispy and golden brown. Cool for 10 minutes before serving. Makes 12 servings.

1 serving: 340 Calories; 14 g Total Fat (6 g Mono, 2 g Poly, 5 g Sat); 20 mg Cholesterol; 54 g Carbohydrate (8 g Fibre, 34 g Sugar); 5 g Protein; 115 mg Sodium

Peach Trifle

Trifle never tasted so good! And this version is perfect for the health conscious family. It has much less fat than traditional trifle, is very good source of vitamin C and is high in protein and potassium. So dig in!

Fresh peaches, cored and peeled	6	6
Sugar	2 tbsp.	30 mL
Egg whites	6	6
Cream of tartar	1/4 tsp.	1 mL
Sugar	1/4 cup	60 mL
Banana, mashed	1	1
Whipping cream	1/2 cup	125 mL
Angel food cake, cut into 1/2 inch (12 mm) slices	1/2 lbs.	225 g
Chopped almonds	1/4 cup	60 mL

Cut peaches into 1/4 inch (12 mm) slices and toss with first amount of sugar.

Combine egg whites and cream of tartar in bowl of a stand mixer. Whip until soft peaks form, then fold in remaining sugar until mixture is firm. You should be able to turn bowl upside down without losing mixture. Fold mashed banana into mixture. Transfer with rubber spatula from mixing bowl to another bowl. Reuse mixing bowl to whip cream until firm. Fold whipped cream into banana mixture and set aside.

Place half of angel food cake slices in a large glass bowl and top with half of peaches, then with a layer of whipped mixture. Repeat layer sequence, and garnish with almonds. Serve chilled. Makes 8 servings.

1 serving: 260 Calories; 8 g Total Fat (3 g Mono, 1 g Poly, 3 g Sat); 15 mg Cholesterol; 45 g Carbohydrate (2 g Fibre, 17 g Sugar); 7 g Protein; 360 mg Sodium

Tip: When separating eggs, be careful that no yolk makes it into your whites or your whites will not whip properly.

Raspberry Crème Brûlée

A French classic revisited. Soft tofu replaces egg yolks to create the dessert's familiar creamy texture with a fraction of the fat. This vegetarian recipe can be made vegan by using soy milk in place of the cream.

Silken tofu	1 lb.	454 g
Whipping cream	1/4 cup	60 mL
Sugar	3/4 cup	175 mL
Ground cloves	1/8 tsp.	0.5 mL
Salt	1/8 tsp.	0.5 mL
Arrowroot	1 1/2 tbsp.	25 mL
Raspberries	40	40
Sugar	2 tbsp.	30 mL

Gently press tofu, removing just a little water, then place in a blender with whipping cream, first amount of sugar, cloves, salt and arrowroot.

Transfer to 8 individual custard cups or small bowls and press 5 raspberries into each cup. Place bowls in a large roasting pan. Pour boiling water around cups so water is a finger width below top of bowls. Carefully transfer roasting pan to 375°F (190°C) oven and bake for 40 minutes or until custard is firm and slightly brown on top. Remove bowls from pan and place in refrigerator for 1 to 2 hours until cool.

Dust top of each custard bowl with remaining sugar. Broil on top rack until sugar begins to caramelize. Let rest for 2 minutes before serving. Makes 8 servings.

1 serving: 190 Calories; 4 g Total Fat (0.5 g Mono, 0 g Poly, 1 g Sat); 5 mg Cholesterol; 34 g Carbohydrate (1 g Fibre, 30 g Sugar); 6 g Protein; 80 mg Sodium

Tip: Be careful when transferring a water-filled dish in or out of the oven, and when closing the oven door. Any shakes can cause the water to spill into the bowls and compromise the custard.

Mocha Layer Cake

A decadent, old-fashioned–looking layer cake with a fraction of the fat. Less than 300 calories for a great big piece! It's so easy to throw together that it will become your go-to cake for special occasions—or just because.

All-purpose flour	1 3/4 cups	425 mL
Sugar	1 cup	250 mL
Baking soda	1 tsp.	5 mL
Salt	1/2 tsp.	2 mL
Hot strong prepared coffee	1 cup	250 mL
Cocoa, sifted if lumpy	1/2 cup	125 mL
1% buttermilk	1/2 cup	125 mL
Egg whites (about 2 large)	1/4 cup	60 mL
Vanilla extract	1 tsp.	5 mL
Cold strong prepared coffee	1 cup	250 mL
Box of instant fat-free chocolate pudding powder (4-serving size)	1	1
Frozen 95% fat-free whipped topping, thawed	3 cups	750 mL

Line bottom of two 8 inch (20 cm) round pans with parchment paper circles. Spray sides with cooking spray. Set aside. Combine first 4 ingredients in large bowl.

Whisk first amount of coffee and cocoa in a small bowl until cocoa is dissolved.

Combine next 3 ingredients in a medium bowl. Stir in coffee mixture. Add to flour mixture. Stir until just combined. Spread evenly in prepared pans. Bake in 350°F (175°C) oven for about 20 minutes until wooden pick inserted in centre of cake comes out clean. Let rest in pans for 10 minutes before inverting onto wire racks to cool completely. Cut each cake in half horizontally to make 4 layers.

For the frosting, beat second amount of coffee and pudding powder in medium bowl for 2 minutes. Add 1 cup (250 mL) whipped topping. Stir until combined. Fold in remaining whipped topping. Chill for 30 minutes. Place 1 cake layer on serving plate. Spread with about 1/2 cup (125 mL) frosting. Repeat with second and third cake layers, spreading about 1/2 cup (125 mL) frosting between each layer. Cover with remaining cake layer. Spread remaining frosting over top and sides of cake. Chill for at least 1 hour. Cuts into 8 wedges.

1 wedge: 280 calories; 2.5 g Total Fat (0.5 g Mono, 0 g Poly, 1 g Sat); 5 mg Cholesterol; 60 g Carbohydrate (3 g Fibre, 30 g Sugar); 6 g Protein; 490 mg Sodium

Index